Everyday Superfoods

Everyday SUPER FOODS

Live **HEALTHIER**

Improve Your **MOOD**

Boost Your **IMMUNITY**

Dr Nandita Iyer

BLOOMSBURY

NEW DELHI • LONDON • OXFORD • NEW YORK • SYDNEY

BLOOMSBURY INDIA
Bloomsbury Publishing India Pvt. Ltd
Second Floor, LSC Building No. 4, DDA Complex, Pocket C – 6 & 7,
Vasant Kunj, New Delhi, 110070

BLOOMSBURY, BLOOMSBURY INDIA and the Diana logo
are trademarks of Bloomsbury Publishing Plc

First published in India 2021
This edition published 2021

ISBN: PB: 978-93-89611-42-7; eBook: 978-93-89611-41-0
2 4 6 8 10 9 7 5 3 1

Typeset in Manipal Technologies Limited
Printed and bound in India by Gopsons Papers Pvt. Ltd., Noida

MIX
Paper | Supporting responsible forestry
FSC® C191020

To my dearest Atri,
who makes the best ginger tea

Contents

1

Our Relationship with Food

The earliest available fossil evidence shows that Homo Sapiens diverged from the earlier Hominin species around 2,00,000 years ago. The Hominins were hunter-gatherers, moving from place to place in search of food. The hunter-gatherer diet was made up of wild plants and animals, but they mostly relied on plants as they were easier to come by and required less effort–except in higher altitudes where there was not much vegetation.

The gathering was done by the women and children, while hunting was typically left to the men. Their foraged diet mainly consisted of fruit, berries, nuts and some wild vegetables, including roots and tubers. The meat came from mostly hunting smaller animals like rabbit, goat or deer, fishing or scavenging the meat of larger animals.

The hunter-gatheres moved about in small groups comprising a few family units. They stayed in temporary shelters until much later, around 20,000 years ago, when they finally started living in stone-built houses[1] in some parts of the world. The foraged plant-based foods and meat provided just enough energy to fuel their high level of physical activity that included climbing trees, hunting, running away from wild animals, walking long distances and so on.

This period continued for around 1,90,000 years till the Neolithic Revolution, which started around 11,000 to 12,000 years ago. During the Neolithic period, humans moved towards settled communities and started to grow crops. This probably started in the Fertile Crescent (present day Middle East) between 10,000 and 8,000 BCE. A settled lifestyle enabled them to experiment with growing plants, which led to a spurt in agriculture followed by selective breeding of crops. This period saw the domestication of plants and animals in different locations around the world. It was also the start of irrigation, deforestation and a narrowing of biodiversity.

The hunter-gatherers used their sense of hearing, sight, taste, touch, and smell to survive the wild and to avoid picking any poisonous foods while foraging. Mindfulness was the key to their survival, and it came to them reflexively. It would not be excessive to say that we humans have almost lost this mindfulness to guide us in our eating habits due to prolonged disuse.

Today, the Aboriginal communities around the world, who predominantly depend on the forests and surrounding nature for their food and livelihood, continue to exercise their senses. However, such communities in the forests of India are also inching towards an urban lifestyle as their foraging and hunting habitat continues to shrink due to deforestation and encroachment of tribal lands[2] to exploit its mineral wealth.

Present-day humans share a multilayered relationship with food

At its most basic, food is a means to counter hunger and keep us alive. When we say '*roti, kapda aur makaan*' (bread, clothes and shelter) are the three basic needs for humans, roti is always on top of that list.

Food is also one of life's joys, be it indulging in a ghee-rich *gaajar ka halwa* (carrot pudding) in the winters, partaking in the wedding feast of a loved one or planning a party menu for your child's birthday. Food offers pleasure to all the five senses.

During the COVID-19 pandemic, many of us have taken a refuge in home cooking. Our favourite comfort foods have been helping us get through through lockdowns and are also fuelling family-bonding over meals.

Thus, it is safe to say that food often swings between the two extremes of sustenance and indulgence. It is the social grease of our present-day lifestyle. It's always 'let's catch up over coffee or a meal' as much as I wish it were catch up over a run in the park. All around the world, food is deeply intertwined with social and cultural life.

Food has also become a trend to keep up with. Cooking, which was earlier seen as a mundane chore, is now seen in a new light as an exciting hobby to pursue. Popular cooking shows like *Masterchef Australia* have brought the fanciest ingredients, equipment, techniques and dishes into our everyday lives and conversations. Even children know culinary terms like croquembouche, al dente, sous vide and chocolate soil. However, food as a trend or hobby is more common in urban households in India.

To quote Hippocrates, 'Let food be thy medicine and medicine be thy food'. Food is also seen as a medicine and as a means to a healthy lifestyle. While it is true that certain foods eaten over a while can lead to some health complications, there are many other foods that prevent as well as alleviate certain other health conditions. Vitamins, minerals, antioxidants, and fibre are some of the components in food that qualify it to be healthy.

However, our relationship with food has become more complicated in today's world. Conflicting theories about foods like ghee, eggs, coconut oil, bread, sugar, milk, etc., leave us confused about our choices. To top this, there are a bunch of new fad diets that catch the fancy of the media and the people ever so often. In the Digital Age, where everything tends to become viral quickly, there is also fake news and clickbait articles providing sensational but utterly unverified information around nutrition, disease prevention, and cures that many innocent people fall for.

Now, there is also a term for an eating disorder in which the person has an unhealthy obsession with eating healthy—Orthorexia. Some of the other common eating disorders that typically start during adolescence include Anorexia Nervosa, Bulimia Nervosa, and Binge eating disorder. All these eating disorders are mental health conditions that require the attention of qualified health professionals and counsellors.

Today, urban lives are hectic and running a kitchen requires a lot of effort. Stocking up on groceries and fresh produce, managing the perishables, serving freshly cooked food at mealtimes, and post-cooking clean-up are just some of the things that need a lot of time and investment.

Historically, managing the kitchen has always been a woman's job. As per a data-backed article from 2019 from Pew Research Centre, 80 per cent of married women in the U.S. households with at least one child under the age of 18 said that they are responsible for buying groceries and prepping meals[3]. As per the India Human Development Survey data quoted in a 2020 paper in the *Journal of Cleaner Production*, the primary cooks in 98 per cent of the households in India are females[4]. Even though women make up a considerable part of the present-day workforce, the sentiment of '*ma ke haath ka khana*' (food from the mother's hands) still exists. Thus, since the beginning of human civilization, there hasn't been much of a change in the gender skew as far as home cooking is concerned.

In many homes, dinner is usually the only meal that the family gets to eat together. Even that is punctuated with or accompanied by distractions from digital screens. In fact, that is true for all mealtimes. Due to this, cooking and eating dinner is a hasty, distracted and mindless exercise for most of us. It is a chore to get done with. This lack of mindfulness towards our food means we rarely pay attention to its quantity, appearance, taste and aroma. This leads to a lack of satiety and an absence of bonding with the food we eat and the people with whom we eat. A structured literature review on the role of mindfulness, mindful eating and intuitive eating in changing eating behaviours concluded that mindful eating was successful in reducing episodes of binge eating, emotional eating, and eating in response to external cues[5]. Mindful eating also resulted in a positive shift in eating habits and led to reduced quantities of food consumed.

The frequency of eating in a day is also an important thing to note. In the Stone Age, humans were used to eating irregularly after long periods of fasting or whenever food became available. Our bodies are still accustomed to this system, given that this way of life covered a long time period, almost 99 per cent of human history.

Today, food is easily available to us all the time – even in the middle of the night! This easy access to food, paired with eating for reasons other than hunger leads to eating too often and too much in a day, both of which go against the principles of how our human bodies have evolved.

Another new invention affecting our relationship with food is the incessant variety of packaged, ready-to-eat snacks that are easily available in supermarkets and online.

High in salt, refined oils, preservatives, and artificial flavours, these calorie-dense, nutrient-poor foods also tend to be very addictive; unfortunately, they have been well-entrenched in our daily diets. The Indian ready-to-eat food industry made over ₹1,900 crores in 2017, and is projected to reach over ₹4,800 crores by 2023. This can be attributed to increasing urbanization and disposable incomes, along with changes in consumers' taste preferences. According to an article in the *Financial Express*[6], since June this year, i.e., in the COVID-19 period, curries, meals, batters, instant mixes, desserts and frozen snacks have seen a 25–30 per cent increase due to a larger number of people cooking at home. While these foods provide a much-needed convenience for families, it is also important to be wary of the nutrient profile of such packaged foods.

Food delivery apps are a big wave in the F&B (Food & Beverage) space. We are now connected to almost every hotel, restaurant, cafe, or a tea stall via a food delivery app. At the touch of a button, food from their kitchens is delivered right at our doorstep. During the COVID-19 pandemic, while restaurants were being forced to shut down, the food delivery business started booming. Even after the restaurants have opened up, people find it safer to order in rather than eating out. The food ordered via these apps is often so discounted that buying from these places is cheaper than buying groceries to cook the same food at home. Not to forget, it's time-saving too. However, it's important to remember that mass-produced food tends to be high in salt and oil with a spice overload to mask any shortcomings in the freshness of ingredients used and the hygiene standards that often cannot be vouched for. There is also the problem of serious environmental damage caused by the quantity of single-use plastic waste generated by food deliveries.

'Don't eat anything your great-great-great-grandmother wouldn't recognize as food.'

Take a minute to ponder over this very simple, yet profound sentence from the modern guru of food wisdom, Michael Pollan. Keeping the word 'great-great-great-grandmother' in mind, I did this interesting exercise where I compared our present-day food habits to that of my great-grandparents'. My maternal great-grandparents are the oldest people I know and have had the privilege of spending time with them well into my adulthood.

There are five things that I remember clearly with respect to them and food:

- Mealtimes were sacrosanct. They stuck to the exact mealtimes every single day—11 a.m. for lunch and 8 p.m. for dinner. There was no multitasking while eating.
- Even though they had moved from their native home in Tamil Nadu to Mumbai in their early 20's, the everyday menu consisted of traditional Tamil-style vegetarian dishes.
- They would hardly ever eat out, except at family weddings or functions.
- They used to eat whatever was local, seasonal and cheap. Food was cooked fresh using these seasonal ingredients and the quantity just enough for the meal. Lack of refrigerators in the early days meant that cooked food was never carried forward to the next day. The dishes were simple and frugal. Money was tight, and wasting it on extravagant foods was never an option.
- Other than the odd biscuit with afternoon tea (that too in their 60's), not much of what they ate came out of a packet. My great-grandfather's favourite teatime snack was a small piece of jaggery with some raw peanuts.

In contrast, our present-day relationship with food looks something like this:

- A screen is quite often a mealtime companion for the whole family. It is a common practice to feed toddlers by showing them their favourite cartoons so they can eat without fuss.
- We eat an overwhelming variety of foods and cuisines in addition to our traditional cuisine.
- Eating out and ordering in is no longer a special occasion but a regular affair.
- We pride ourselves on eating foods from around the world, which is, usually, off-season and expensive.
- We regularly eat highly processed foods, i.e., far from their natural form.

2

Improving Your Relationship with Food

> *[T]he quality of the food we put into our bodies matters because it drives our gene function, metabolism and overall health.'*
>
> – Dr Mark Hyman

Why is our relationship with food important?

Over the last few decades, the focus of medical research has been on life-saving surgeries and treatments. The developments in the field of medicine and better healthcare facilities (mostly in urban areas) have led to an increased life expectancy. In 2016, the average global life expectancy was 72 years[1]. However, coupled with this increasing life expectancy, there has also been an increase in the incidence of chronic diseases such as, cardiovascular disease, cancer, chronic respiratory disease, and diabetes. Having a constant problem-solving approach does not work when it comes to health; prevention of disease and maintenance of health needs the same amount of focus. Recently, the medical fraternity and people at large are realizing that along with a longer life span, we need a better quality of life. As per a World

Health Organization (WHO) report[2], at least 80 per cent of premature heart disease, stroke and type 2 diabetes, and 40 per cent of cancer can be prevented through a healthy diet, regular physical activity, and avoidance of tobacco products. A sedentary lifestyle combined with our dietary habits is one of the biggest reasons for many of our problems today. So, improving our lifestyle and diet can help us enjoy a better quality of life.

Medical research shows a strong connection between chronic inflammation and heart disease, diabetes, cancer, arthritis and other chronic diseases. According to an article in *Harvard Health Publishing*[3], the best approach to prevent chronic inflammation in the body is to maintain a healthy weight, choose a good diet, get plenty of sleep, and exercise regularly. Cutting down on simple sugars and processed foods and eating more antioxidant-rich foods are two good dietary practices that can prevent or reduce chronic inflammation. This, in turn, can reduce the incidence of chronic diseases.

While staying active is also very important, all the physical exercise cannot compensate for a poor diet. Table 2.1 shows how a healthy relationship with food and eating good quality nutrient-rich foods makes us look better, feel better, and age better.

Table 2.1: The Effects of a Healthy Relationship with Food

Look better	Healthy skin and hair	Almonds, mushroom, tomatoes, spinach, bell peppers, legumes
Feel better	Better digestion, energy, immunity, fitness levels and mood	Beans, leafy greens, yoghurt, overnight oats, dark chocolate, beetroot

Age better	Longevity along with a good quality of life. Decreased chance of developing chronic diseases, better energy levels, remaining mentally agile, staying mobile and independent.	Whole grains, nuts, seeds, beans, red grapes, tomatoes, green tea, garlic, ginger

Making smart choices about food also gives us more productive days, more energy to devote to our life and work, fewer sicknesses, and savings on medical bills. It makes us better role models for our children and future generations, who learn how to sustain a happy and healthy relationship with food and make better food choices for themselves.

How to improve your relationship with food

I. Reflection and awareness

Thinking deeply about the food we consume and connecting with our food are the first steps we can take towards making positive changes in our diet and our lifestyle. Nowadays, we are becoming more aware of our damaging food habits, our addiction to processed foods, and the negative impact on the environment due to our poor choices in the last few decades. Many of us are in the midst of re-examining our roots and our food choices. Giving a thought to the provenance of the ingredients we cook with and the people (or factories) behind them is a step in the right direction.

Food awareness helps navigate the muddy waters of information and choice overload. It is important to be aware of the impact of the food we eat on our body and the environment. Taking a closer look at our daily diet and making small sustainable changes where required can manoeuvre us in the right direction–towards a healthier us.

Some of the simple questions you can ask yourself to be aware are:

1. Am I eating a balanced meal?
2. Am I eating enough fruits and vegetables?
3. Am I taking the time to sit down for my meals and chew my food well?
4. How often am I eating out?

II. Empowering with knowledge

Acquiring knowledge about ingredients and cooking techniques is a continuous process. You can take courses, attend workshops, and follow genuine sources of information on the internet to learn about nutrient-rich foods to incorporate them into your daily diet. Staying away from clickbait and sensational information around nutrition or anything that promises instant results is equally imperative.

Eating a diet rich in superfoods is like investing in well-performing stocks. They pack the most nutrition per calorie and have a proven track record in providing many health benefits. The chapter 'The Superfood Compendium' on page 25 is a good place to start. If you absolutely must buy processed foods, reading food labels is critical to check for sugar, sodium and trans-fats. This enables one to choose a better product from those available.

III. Home cooking with family involvement

Cooking healthy meals at home on a daily basis can be made easier by planning menus in advance, weekly meal prep, and making cooking a fun family activity with each member chipping in a little bit. This decreases the dependence on ready-to-eat packaged foods and takeaways.

It is good to include children in shopping for fresh produce or groceries and in simple cooking prep so that they have a head start in learning about food and healthy eating. You can read a lot more about this in the 'Getting Practical with Superfoods' chapter on page 149.

IV. Reducing intake of processed foods

The best way to eat is to choose foods closest to their natural form, i.e., in an unprocessed or minimally processed form. Some of the examples are: having a banana instead of banana bread; using butter, ghee or cold-pressed oil instead of refined oil; eating homemade potato wedges instead of packaged potato chips; opting for whole grains instead of breakfast cereals, and making homemade roti instead of buying commercial breads.

The journey from corn to cornflakes

- The process of manufacturing cornflakes involves peeling and removal of the endosperm of corn kernels. They are then cooked, dried, rolled, toasted, cooled, and finally packed.
- Quite a few additives such as salt, sweeteners, flavouring agents, preservatives, colouring agents, and yeast are added to the grains while processing.
- Vitamins, like Thiamine, are also added to the cornflakes to make up for what is lost due to processing on high heat.
- Chemical preservatives are added to keep the finished product from going stale or rancid, which allows it to be in the distribution chains and our kitchen shelves for months.

It is okay to include processed ingredients obtained via pressing, milling or grinding which are used to get oils, *poha*, atta, etc., to cook dishes. This is different from processed or ultra-processed foods that have added salt, sugar, fats, artificial flavours, colours, preservatives, stabilizers, etc.

Some common highly processed foods include,

- White sugar
- Breakfast cereals
- Commercially sold bread
- Commercially sold biscuits and snacks
- Processed cheese
- Juice from tetra packs
- Refined oils
- Polished white rice
- Refined flours
- Instant coffee
- Potato chips
- Microwave popcorn
- Aerated drinks
- Instant noodles
- Instant soups from a packet
- Energy bars
- Commercially sold chocolate bars
- Ketchup
- Frozen desserts

V. *Retraining tastebuds*

Retraining your tastebuds will help break the cycle of dependence on processed foods. It also makes your palate more accepting of a variety of healthy ingredients and foods. This is quite like the weaning period of a baby once they turn six months old and new foods are introduced to them one after the other.

Cut out on sweet foods that add sugars or sugar alternatives like honey, jaggery, artificial sweeteners, etc., during this transition phase. Avoid processed foods, like packaged snacks high in salt and artificial flavours. The addiction to salty and sweet tastes can be broken by introducing more of the sour, umami and bitter flavours in our food.

Sour: Lime, tamarind, *kokum*, fruit vinegar, green mangoes, amchoor and fermented foods like yoghurt, kombucha, kimchi
Umami: Sautéed mushrooms, roasted or cooked tomatoes, soy sauce
Bitter: Variety of dark green leafy vegetables, bitter gourd, teasel gourd, turmeric, fenugreek, grapefruit

Salads are a good way to combine the ingredients of these flavours close to their natural form. Try to include a salad made using fresh greens, veggies, fruits, nuts, and a dressing as a part of every meal. In just one or two weeks, the tastebuds will adjust to a lower salt and sugar level in food.

VI. Think about the environment

Even if you are careful about the food you eat, a lot is left to be desired from the quality of ingredients and produce. Due to industrialized agriculture, fresh produce may not have an optimum level of nutrients the body needs to keep itself in good health. In many large farms, the soil has been stripped of its nutrients over the years, and uncontrolled usage of pesticides and fertilizers has further affected the quality of the soil and, thereby, the produce harvested from it.

Other factors, such as global warming, erratic rainfall, erosion of soil, etc., all indirectly affect the quality of food that is cultivated. There is also reduced biodiversity due to selective cultivation of plant species – a narrow range of produce is being used today while many others are being neglected. These are all things to consider when we look at farming for food.

Choosing foods that are gently grown without stripping the soil of nutrients or polluting groundwater with pesticides, etc., is better for the body and the planet. Fortunately, there are many minimally processed organic foods and conscious food brands entering the market. Farmers' markets, interest in the origin of ingredients, organic kitchen gardening, a renewed love for native Indian ingredients, and traditional cookware are also on the rise.

Kickstart a better relationship with food

A food diary

- The two-step programme
  - ◊ Zero processed foods
  - ◊ Five senses invested in food

Keep a completely honest food diary for three days in which you write down every single thing you eat and drink, along with the time and the source of the food. Also, note down why you ate what you ate; for example, were you hungry, bored or sad?

Table 2.2: A Sample Diary Entry

Time	Food/Drink	Source	Why?
9 a.m.	Banana	Natural	Hungry
11 a.m.	Digestive biscuits	Packet	Bored
1 p.m.	Rice-dal-vegetables	Home-cooked	Hungry, mealtime
5 p.m.	Coconut water; Salted peanuts	Natural; Processed/ from a packet	Hungry

Before bedtime, audit your food intake during the day and make a note of how much processed food you consumed. You can also do this for a week to get a better idea of your dietary habits.

Doing this process diligently will make you aware of how you eat. This can also be done on one of the many food tracker apps, which will also give you the percentage of carbohydrates, protein and fats in your daily diet.

Once you have an idea of your food habits and diet, you are ready for the two-step programme to kickstart your journey towards healthier eating.

Step one: Zero processed foods

For a week, try to not eat anything that comes out of a packet. If you follow this step diligently, you will end up cooking more meals from scratch and snack on natural foods, like fruits and nuts. Keep a record similar to the food diary on all the foods that you consume. Do not worry about calories or the composition of foods as long as they are close to their natural form. It is almost impossible to overeat unprocessed foods or get an unhealthy craving for them. Ever heard of anyone who had a craving for broccoli or binged on bananas?

In addition to this, make a note of how you feel at the end of each day, i.e., your energy levels, any reduction in earlier symptoms of poor health such as allergies or skin eruptions, aches and pains, etc.

Step two: Five senses invested in food

Reinvest your senses in the food you eat. Bond with the ingredients used to prepare the dish in front of you using your senses of touch, smell, sight, sound, and taste. Enjoy the feel of a well-kneaded dough, the faintly sour aroma of fermented idli batter, the visual beauty of a colourful fresh salad, the sharp crackle of cumin and mustard seeds spluttering for a *tadka,* and the taste of a perfectly sweet and sour Nagpur orange.

You will start noticing these things when you apply mindfulness to cooking and eating. Being mindful enables us to make better choices, slows us down, and makes us enjoy our food wholeheartedly. Mindful eating also gives us satiety from much less, as we are more conscious of our appetite and hunger.

Tips to eat more mindfully

- Before eating, ask yourself if you are really hungry or is it thirst, boredom or something else?
- Plate your food so that it looks appealing. Serve yourself a smaller portion to start with. You can always get seconds if you are still hungry.
- Put all digital devices out of reach during mealtimes.
- Sit down to eat—be it a full meal or a snack.
- Take a moment to be grateful for the food in front of you.
- Take small bites and chew each bite well. Let a few seconds pass before you take the next bite. This intentional slowing down will help make slow eating a habit.
- While eating, focus on the colours, textures and flavours of the food. This will also help slow down the eating process.
- Make light and happy conversations with people around you. Inflammatory and stressful topics are best left off the dinner table.
- Towards the end, check in with yourself if you are full or if you need a second serving.
- Don't go by the set norms of ordering multiple courses of food in a restaurant. Order as per your appetite. Even a single course may suffice your appetite.

3

Enriching Your Diet with Superfoods

After re-examining your current diet, reducing the intake of processed foods, and reinvesting your senses into food, the next step is to gradually introduce foods that have a better nutrient profile into your daily meals, i.e., enriching your diets with superfoods.

What is a superfood?

Take a minute to think deeply about this word – 'superfood' – that is thrown around like confetti by the media, health fiends, gym trainers, the #cleaneating tribes on Instagram, and innumerable food brands. Given how the term has been overused, one would think a superfood is like a superhero – a nut, a seed, or a berry wearing a cape, flying around in a tiny jet, rescuing human beings from supervillains like heart diseases, cancer and diabetes while making good on their wishes for great skin, a fighting-fit immunity and longevity. Even though this is not entirely fantasy, it is quite far from the truth. The latter may sound disheartening and may make you question the very raison d'être for this book, but let me explain.

No single superfood has the magical powers to transform our lives and health all by itself. The human body is a very complex machine and the solutions to a healthy and long life cannot be as simple as eating a particular food or swallowing a pill of extracts.

So, if not saving the world, one person at a time, what do superfoods do exactly?

Merriam-Webster Dictionary defines the prefix "super" as 'over and above: higher in quantity, quality or degree', which means that the term 'superfood' is a food of very high quality. In the book, *Diet Cults* by Matt Fitzgerald[1], it is mentioned that the oldest usage of the term 'superfood' was in a poem published in a Jamaican newspaper as a reference to wine. The second-oldest known usage of the word 'superfood' was in 1949 – in an article in a Canadian newspaper referring to the nutritional qualities of a muffin!

Today, seven decades later, it is a radically overused buzzword. The term superfood is a marketing ploy used by health food brands and stores to woo us. It is an unregulated licence to sell us overpriced food. If I had to describe superfoods without succumbing to superlatives, I would say that they comprise of foods that are a concentrated source of one or more nutrients, such as vitamins, minerals, and antioxidants. Due to their nutrient density, these foods help boost general health, immunity and longevity, or are known for specific benefits, such as cancer prevention or blood sugar management.

It would not be wrong to call them 'smart foods' because choosing foods with more nutrient density is a smarter choice for good health.

Questions to ask before buying a superfood

I. Is it easily available?

Even if a food item has an enviable nutritional profile, it needs to be easily available for it to become a part of your daily diet. It is easy to feel disheartened when you google 'top superfoods' and eight out of ten foods recommended by a US-based website are either not easily available in India or are very expensive. For example, blueberries and blackberries are often sold in exorbitantly priced tiny boxes on the shelves of gourmet food stores. Since these are flown in from thousands of kilometres away, they are bound to be priced accordingly. However, foods like *amla*, tomatoes and green moong are always around for the picking. So, choose wisely.

II. Is it local?

This is also a part of the previous question, but we need to address this in some more detail. Sometimes, due to the sheer marketing money behind a product, apples grown in the U.S. appear more easily available to us than the Bangalore blue grapes grown locally.

Eating food from thousands of miles away comes with its own problems. The carbon footprint that comes with such food is a blot on sustainable eating. Also, transporting food takes anywhere from days to weeks, depending on the distances involved and the mode of transportation; and delicate nutrients like water-soluble vitamins are prone to get affected over a few days, with exposure to heat and light. Additionally, the transportation and import duties make this a very expensive proposition.

When quinoa's popularity as a superfood skyrocketed everywhere in the world, it became overpriced and unaffordable to the South Americans themselves, for whom it is a staple food. This is the downside to mindlessly approximating superfoods from another culture. India, being a large country with diverse geographies and food habits, has so many more local superfoods to offer, such as the millets in Karnataka and the amaranth in Uttaranchal.

III. Is it cultivated responsibly?

When we eat a superfood for its nutritional benefits, it makes no sense if the liver has to work overtime removing the pesticides and other chemicals that may have been used in its cultivation. Anything that is industrially produced in the world cannot qualify as a superfood. A food that is produced in massive quantities depletes the soil of its nutrients, thereby making the food not very beneficial to us in the long run. Now that the Industrial Revolution has ensured that people are fed, maybe it is time to look at quality over quantity.

IV. Is it seasonal?

It has been proven that foods in season are chock-full of nutrients as compared to their off-season counterparts. As tempting as a mango in December may seem, you can eat it to satiate your craving but you can't exactly count it as a good nutritional choice. On the other hand, frozen fruits with no other additives are a better choice because these are plucked during peak ripeness and, therefore, retain a good level of nutrients.

V. Is it affordable?

The criteria 'local' and 'easily available' do take care of this question to some extent. It is indeed a matter of privilege to be able to spend time, money and efforts on eating healthy. Even for most of the privileged, it is not feasible to include expensive foods in meals on a daily basis. There are plenty of local superfoods that can compete with the nutritional profile of expensive imported varieties.

Chapter 5, 'The Superfood Compendium', of this book is a testament to that.

VI. Is it unprocessed or minimally processed?

Ideally, a superfood should not come out of a packet. However, concessions can be made for a few processes, such as milling, grinding, and freezing. Reading the nutrition label on the packaging is a good indicator of how processed the food is. A short list of ingredients with the superfood ingredient listed first, no added sugar, salt, fillers and preservatives are some of the pointers to keep in mind while checking the labels. Even if the superfood is listed as one of the ingredients, do check how much of it is actually present in the product. 'After going through processing, does the finished product still qualify as a superfood?' or 'if fruits or vegetables that are considered superfoods are processed and packaged, do they still qualify as superfoods?' – these are a couple of questions you should ask of all the products jostling for space in health food stores with the words 'superfood' written on them in big jazzy fonts.

Should juices be a part of a minimally processed diet? The best way to eat fruits and vegetables is to eat them whole, but if you are getting your share of fibre from a variety of vegetables and fruits in meals through the day, juicing vegetables and greens along with a fruit like apple, pineapple or orange for natural sweetness is a good way to get a concentrated shot of vitamins in a pleasant-tasting drink.

Superfood mantras

- Superfoods are not magic pills – Having the occasional superfood smoothie or superfood energy ball alone will not change your health report. Eating healthy needs to be accompanied by an overall healthy lifestyle and it needs a lifelong commitment.
- Superfoods will not rescue you from a bad diet – Even if you eat all the superfoods in the world, you still need to watch the rest of your diet. If the mainstay of your diet is processed food, then superfoods will not rescue you from the impact of the not-so-super foods.
- Superfoods are not calorie-free – Superfoods have calories too, albeit the better kind of calories. Moderation is important even when eating superfoods.
- Superfoods must be cooked right – Make efforts to understand the best way to cook and eat each superfood to minimize nutrient loss and maximize absorption. For example, whole grains like millets or legumes, like green moong could do with soaking, sprouting, fermenting or a combination of all three.
- Seek a wider variety of superfoods – Eating a variety of superfoods ensures that we get a variety of micronutrients from our diet. Encouraging biodiversity in our diet is also good for the environment.
- Balanced diet + superfoods is the way to go – To sum it up, eat a balanced diet that includes everyday superfoods in everyday dishes to stay healthy.

4

The Superfood Compendium

This chapter includes some of the nutrient-rich foods that qualify as superfoods, with a focus on some of their key nutrients. It also includes easy ways to include these superfoods in our daily diet. All the superfoods that have made it to this compendium are rich in antioxidants, locally available in most parts of India, and reasonably affordable. All of these foods provide innumerable health benefits when consumed on a regular basis.

Incorporating every kind of superfood in this compendium is beyond the scope of this book, but I do hope this is a good starting point to 'superfood-ize' your diet.

AMARANTH / AMARANTHUS CRUENTUS

The name amaranth is common to 60 different species of Amaranthus. It is derived from the Greek word amárantos, which means 'never-fading'. The stunning pink-red tasselled flowers retain their beauty even when harvested and dried. The same name goes for both the green leafy vegetable as well as the edible seed. Amaranth is considered a pseudograin (i.e., seeds that can be used as grains and ground to a flour) as it does not belong to the grass family like true cereals. This 8,000-year-old seed has a fascinating history. It was originally a part of the Incan, Mayan and Aztec civilizations, and fell out of favour when it was banned by the conquerors for religious reasons[1].

Amaranth is a hardy crop that grows like a weed, even in trying conditions. It is also native to Mongolia, Nepal, the Himalayan regions in India, and the hilly terrain in south India. It is a native crop in Uttarakhand, where the flour of the amaranth is used to make rotis, and the roasted (or popped) grains are eaten as a snack. It is known by different names in India, including *chaulai*, *ramdana* and *rajgira*. Earlier, it was mainly grown as a barter crop to exchange for goods from traders. However, the cultivation of Amaranth has increased since 2008 or 2009 due to the steady increase in demand for the plant.[2]

In China, amaranth is grown in the mountainous regions, and is called *tien-shu-tze* (millet from heaven). The popped seeds are eaten with hot sugar syrup. In the amaranth season, some African societies get nearly 25 per cent of their daily protein by consuming these leaves.

Nutrition in amaranth

Amaranth seeds are rich in protein, calcium, and fibre. The seeds are a good source of the amino acid lysine, which is deficient in cereals. However, Amaranth is deficient in the amino acid leucine, which is present in cereals. So combining amaranth with a cereal and a pulse is a good way to get all the essential amino acids in our diet. This combination provides a source of complete protein for vegans and vegetarians. It is also a good source of manganese, magnesium, phosphorus, and iron. Amaranth, in the form of flour (*rajgira*), is one of the foods eaten during fasts in north and west India. It is an excellent source of energy and antioxidants. It contains more protein, calcium, fibre, and iron, compared to rice.

It is also an excellent choice for postmenopausal women to prevent osteoporosis as 100 grams of cooked amaranth has 389 milligram of calcium.

One cup of cooked amaranth provides over 100 per cent of the daily requirement of manganese, which is an important micronutrient for brain function.

How to use

Raw amaranth is inedible, and anti-nutrient compounds, such as phytic acid and tannins present in the seed can prevent the absorption of vital nutrients such as minerals.

Soaking, sprouting, and fermenting are some of the ways to reduce the effects of anti-nutrients.

Here are some of the ways to use amaranth.

1. Soak the grains overnight, drain and keep for two to three days to allow sprouting. Cook sprouted amaranth grains with rice and *tur* dal to make a nutritious *khichdi*. This dish is a complete protein, providing all the essential amino acids.
2. Lightly toasted amaranth can be simmered in milk along with raw sugar to make *kheer*. Amaranth also acts as a thickener, giving a rich and creamy consistency to the *kheer*.
3. Soak amaranth grains for four to five hours. Drain and boil in a pot of water until grains are just cooked but not mushy. Use this cooked amaranth to bulk up salads and soups.
4. Popped amaranth grains can be made into *chikkis, laddoos,* or used in a granola mix.
5. Substitute a portion of regular flour with amaranth flour in baking to increase the protein levels in the dish.

Where to buy

You will find amaranth grains in organic or health food stores. It is also commonly available online, both on Amazon and platforms selling health foods. Do check the label to understand the region it is grown in.

Similar to quinoa, amaranth, now a high-end superfood, is increasingly becoming unavailable to the very people who grow them, as farmers would rather sell it at a higher price and buy cheaper grains for their own consumption. So, I would not recommend totally switching to amaranth. Treat it as one of the grains to include in your weekly menus.

While this entry is about the seeds, amaranth greens are also an important superfood. They are easily available in markets around India during the summer. Amaranth leaves are mild in flavour and easy to cook into a variety of dishes, across cuisines. They have more iron than spinach.

When you buy a bunch of green or red amaranth, sort out the tender small-sized leaves for a mixed salad, use the larger and more mature leaves for a stir-fry or add to dal or sambar or sauté with garlic and add to pasta. The leaves can also be made into a pesto sauce – blend blanched leaves with toasted almonds, garlic, salt and olive oil.

When making sambar, the stems of the amaranth plant can be chopped and cooked along with the dal. In Bangladesh, a variety of amaranth is cultivated for the stems alone!

AMLA / PHYLLANTHUS EMBLICA

Reaching out from the terrace to pluck *amla* from trees, and biting into the mouth-puckeringly sour fruit are fond memories from my childhood. Drinking water after eating *amla* and experiencing the magic (or chemistry) of sweet-tasting water was always fun. Given how *amla* has the most powerful antioxidants, it has the right to be number one on every top superfoods list, especially in India where it is freely available.

Amla has a unique flavour profile, combining sour, astringent, and bitter. Although it's an acquired taste, it can help our taste-buds take a break from excessive sugar and salt consumption. The largest cultivation of *amla* in the world is in Pratapgarh, Uttar Pradesh. It is also grown in Gujarat, Rajasthan, and Maharashtra. The peak season for harvest is between mid-September and mid-December.

Nutrition in *amla*

Amla is one of the most antioxidant-rich foods with over 50 times the antioxidant capacity in blueberries.

Due to the presence of antioxidant compounds like gallic acid, gallotannin, ellagic acid, and corilagin, which prevent high blood sugar and other diabetes-associated complications, *amla* has a natural anti-diabetic effect[3]. Chromium in *amla* also helps in blood sugar management in diabetics by helping the cells absorb glucose.

The polyphenol tannins and flavonoids in *amla* are said to possess both cancer preventive[4] and anti-tumour properties.

Traditionally, *amla* has been used for its anti-inflammatory and pain relief properties. The anti-inflammatory effect also extends to the liver. Some of the antioxidant compounds protect the liver from the cytotoxic effects of alcohol, and common medications like paracetamol.

Amla is also one of the richest dietary sources of vitamin C. Smokers, who need to consume more vitamin C due to increased oxidative stress and therefore lower plasma levels of the vitamin, could do with the extra boost from *amla*. Additionally, *amla* is added to many skin products due to the effect of vitamin C on skin health[5].

How to use

1. Eating *amla* raw is one of the best ways to consume it. However, biting into an extremely tart fruit is not easy for people who cannot tolerate very sour flavours. Cutting it into smaller pieces, grating it into yoghurt, or adding it to a mixed vegetable and fruit juice could be a good place to start.
2. Adding chopped *amla* to green chutneys instead of adding lemon, along with a pinch of jaggery to balance out the flavours is also a great way to consume more of this fruit.
3. Cooked *amla* (by either boiling on the stovetop or pressure cooking) along with the cooking juices can be mashed and used as a base to make rasam.
4. Lightly steamed *amla* can be broken into its segments, then tossed in a little oil and pickle masala to make an instant pickle.

Preserving the goodness of amla

Due to a short season of availability and the extremely high nutritional value of *amla*, Indian cuisine has numerous ways to preserve them for use around the year.

- The simplest method is to store *amla* in brine. The Brined *amla* can be eaten as is with a meal or it can be coarsely ground with coconut and spices and mixed into yoghurt to make raita. It can also be sliced up and added to a salad or blended with oil and flavourings to make a salad dressing.

- Segments of *amla* can be sun-dried and used as a mouth freshener and digestive (*amla* supari). A sweetened dried version is available in the markets.
- Whole *amlas* can also be preserved in honey for year-round use.
- There are many recipes for *amla* pickles from different parts of India. The Andhra-style *amla* pickle along with some of the pickle's oil is eaten with steamed rice.
- *Amla* is also made into a *murabba* or a preserve with sugar or jaggery. This tastes very good with rotis and parathas, or as a sweet and sour relief to a spicy dish.
- *Amla's* superfood properties have also been harnessed in the popular Ayurvedic preparation, *chyavanprash*, a medicinal fudge made from a mix of 50 odd herbs and spices that is said to be very good for immunity.
- In powder form, *amla* is one of the three fruits that go into Triphala, the Ayurvedic preparation which is said to help the immune system and in digestion.

AVOCADO / PERSEA AMERICANA

My first brush with avocado was at a farmhouse in Talegaon in 2003. The host at the farmhouse told me she fed her toddler mashed avocado instead of butter on toast. Later, in 2005, I had my first guacamole at an authentic Mexican restaurant named *Dos Caminos* in New York City. A molcajete (a traditional Mexican mortar and pestle) sat at the centre of the table, indicating that guacamole was the hero of their menu. Then, I moved to Bengaluru in 2011, where 'butter fruit' made a regular appearance in the local markets, so did other varieties from the farms in and around Chikmagalur and Coorg.

In south India, avocados are known as butter fruit. Many independent homes in old localities of Bengaluru and Mysuru have avocado trees growing in their compounds. The extreme weather conditions, hot dry winds and frost in the northern parts of India are not conducive to the growth of avocado. Given the general preference for sweeter fruits, avocados are not very popular as a fruit to be eaten on its own. Locally, it is used in milkshakes, as a thickening agent to lend a creamy texture.

Nutrition in avocados

Avocados are the highest in calories among all other fruits, at 245 calories per 100 grams (compare this with 32 calories per 100 grams in strawberries). Over 80 per cent of the calories of the avocado are from fats. The fat content and composition in avocados are comparable to those found in olive oil. These fats are heart-healthy monounsaturated fats, especially oleic acid. Eating a portion of avocado with a meal helps in the absorption of fat-soluble vitamins (A, D, E and K), even if your meal contains no added fats.

Avocados are rich in dietary fibre. Different varieties have a varying percentage of fibre. For example, a medium-sized California avocado has a total fibre count of 9.2 grams while a similar-sized Florida avocado has nearly 17 grams of fibre.

Given the high percentage of healthy fats, very low glycemic index or GI (a number that indicates how fast the body converts the carbohydrates in food into blood glucose), high fibre, satiating capacity, and insulin regulation properties, avocados are excellent for diabetics[6]. The regular consumption of avocado also reduces the risk of metabolic syndrome[7] (such as, high blood pressure, high blood sugar, and excess body fat around the waist).

Avocados are good for heart health due to the presence of monounsaturated fatty acids, antioxidants from carotenoids, vitamins E and C, and the anti-inflammatory effect from the phytosterols and flavonoids.

How to use

Avocados are best eaten sliced with a drizzle of extra virgin olive oil, a sprinkle of coarse salt and black pepper. Here are some other ways you can eat avocados.

1. Pair the avocado's mild butter flavour with punchy ingredients like rocket or a mustardy dressing (*kasundi*), or with some mustard oil in salads.
2. Use avocados to make creamy dressings by blending it along with yoghurt, garlic, chilli flakes and lemon juice.
3. Use ripe avocados in smoothies instead of ice cream.
4. Use avocado to make creamy vegan desserts like chocolate mousse.
5. Use chopped avocado as a garnish over a Mexican bean soup or over a plate of nachos.
6. Make guacamole-like dips, in combination with white beans or any other cooked beans.
7. The creamy, soft consistency of the avocado makes for good baby food.

I had a chance to ask a few avocado-related questions to Pranoy Thipaiah from Kerehaklu farms in Chikmagalur, where avocado trees are grown as companion plants in his coffee plantation.

How did avocados come to India?

The avocado's origins are in South and Central America. They were introduced to the rest of the world through the Columbian exchange in the 15th century, along with other ingredients like chillies, tomatoes, and potatoes. Over several decades, avocados have acclimatized to the local environments of India which have cooler climates, such as Chikmagalur, Kodaikanal and Coorg in the south, and some parts of Sikkim. Some of the varieties grown in India are Purple, Green, Pinkerton, Hall, and Reed.

Avocado varieties that do better in India are Gwen and Zutano. The ones frequently found in marketplaces in India are all different breeds, and not a particular variety. The ones found in Indian supermarkets that are often rock hard and stony are the Reed variety.

Given that a tree produces a glut of fruit in season, why are they so expensive?
Farmers usually don't have avocado orchards. Avocados are companion plants, grown along with a main crop like coffee. The demand for avocados has gone up, thanks to increasing awareness about its health benefits and its use in restaurants and cafes. Farmers are playing to the rising demand for this fruit in the cities and are trying to get a fair price for the produce. In Chikmagalur, in 2018, they were sold at ₹60-80 per kilogram. In 2019, they are sold at nearly double the price.

The avocado ripening process is the subject of many internet jokes. Is it really that difficult to get them to ripen and catch them at the perfect ripe stage?
Avocados on the tree remain hard and they start to soften only after they are harvested. They need to be harvested at the correct stage of maturity, using a fruit picker. Fruits harvested by shaking the tree are prone to bruising in the later ripening stage, leading to uneven ripening and even to rotting. Wrapping the fruits in newspaper or brown paper ensures even ripening. The skin turns dark brown or black on ripening, after which the fruit needs to be refrigerated. Keeping it with ripening bananas or tomatoes releases ethylene dioxide that speeds up the ripening process.

BELL PEPPERS / CAPSICUM ANNUUM GROUP

Bell peppers are grown in a variety of vibrant colours, not just the popular yellow, orange, green, and red, but also purple, black, chocolate brown, and white. In most parts of India, green bell peppers are easily available and affordable. Given the rising popularity of cooking Italian and other international cuisines at home, many supermarkets have started selling red, yellow, and orange bell peppers.

Bell peppers belong to the nightshade family, which also includes potatoes, chillies, eggplants, and tomatoes. Their sweet flavour comes from the presence of natural sugars and a complete absence of capsaicinoids, a compound that is responsible for the heat in chillies. Bell peppers have a score of zero on the Scoville scale, which is an indicator of heat (spiciness) in chillies. Like chillies, bell peppers are also native to South Americas.

Including green bell peppers in your diet contributes to the green vegetable quota for the day. The yellow and orange bell peppers, like other fruits and vegetables in this colour, are rich in carotenoids. Carotenoids are plant pigments and a type of phytonutrients that are powerful antioxidants. In general, most children seem to love the coloured bell peppers because of their use in pastas and pizzas, which are two dishes they don't mind eating anytime!

I was once adventurous enough to attempt growing bite-sized chocolate-coloured bell peppers in my kitchen garden. However, the Bengaluru weather wasn't suitable for the plant, and it gave up on me after producing one or two tiny bell peppers. While trying to grow bell peppers of different colours, I realized that all of them start off as green and that the red ones are more ripe than the green bell peppers.

While buying bell peppers, choose the ones that are heavy for their size, have a blemish-free skin, and a fresh-looking stem end.

Nutrition in bell peppers

Bell peppers are very low in calories, giving maximum nutrition per calorie. Extremely rich in vitamin C, just a cup of sliced bell pepper (<100 grams) provides over 150 per cent of your daily required vitamin C at just 30 calories. Vitamin C plays a vital role in scavenging for and destroying free radicals, reducing blood pressure, preventing heart disease, improving absorption of iron, and boosting immunity and skin health. All those benefits can be attained from just half a bell pepper in your salad bowl!

Bell peppers are a good source of vitamins A (mainly seen in red bell peppers) and B6. Green bell peppers provide over 300 mcg of the carotenoids lutein and zeaxanthin, which are important for the protection of the retina and macula from damage, thereby protecting eye health. Vitamin B6 plays an important role in the formation of red blood cells.

Bell peppers are also a decent source of fibre in the diet.

How to use

1. Bell peppers can be eaten raw, either in salads or with dips like hummus. Finely chopped bell peppers along with tomatoes, onions and chillies can be made into a salsa.
2. Bell peppers can be roasted in the oven using olive oil and a sprinkle of salt. Roasted bell peppers make for a good addition to salads too.
3. Bell peppers can be directly grilled on a flame until charred. The skin is peeled and the flesh can be used in dips like *muhammara* and hummus.

4. Using a mix of bell peppers adds a lot of colour to salads, pizzas and pies. These can be used raw or lightly pan-fried according to preference.
5. The cavity of a halved bell pepper makes it an ideal vegetable for stuffing. Choose from ingredients like rice, minced vegetables, potatoes, tofu, paneer and cheese paired with herbs and spices; either pan cook or roast the stuffed bell pepper in an oven.
6. Indian cuisine has many recipes that use bell peppers. It is popularly mixed into a dry curry with paneer, tomatoes and onions, which is eaten with rotis. In south Indian cuisine, capsicum *gojju* in Karnataka and *sambar* in Tamil Nadu are two of the many dishes that are prepared with bell peppers.

If you are a gardening enthusiast, bell peppers are one of the vegetables you can try growing from the seeds found in the vegetable itself. To do this, separate the seeds from the placenta, wash them and allow them to dry on a cloth in the shade for two to three days. Sow the dried seeds in a small cup filled with compost and potting mix. Once four to six true leaves appear, the seedlings can be transferred to a bigger pot or to the soil.

BLACK-EYED PEAS / VIGNA UNGUICULATA

There is some controversy surrounding the origin of black-eyed peas. According to the book, *Beans: A History,* by Ken Albala, opinions regarding its place of origin are divided between West Africa, Ethiopia and Asia. Archaeological evidence from the Chad Basin in Africa suggests that black-eyed peas were domesticated and cultivated as early as 1200 BCE, along with pearl millets. In his book, Albala also mentions that the earliest recorded instance of its use is from India, albeit as fodder.

Black-eyed peas came to the Americas along with the slaves. They are used extensively in southern American cuisine; for example, Hoppin' John is a traditional soul food dish made on new year's day using black-eyed peas, rice and bacon, along with vegetables. In the Caribbean cuisine, black-eyed peas are consumed as beans, as ground batter for fritters (known as *accara*), and as flour.

Also called cowpeas, black-eyed peas are fairly popular in present-day Indian cuisine. In the north, it is called *lobia* or *rongi* and is made into a curry. In Maharashtra, it is called *chawli* and is made into a similar curry called *usal* or *amti* to be had with rice or rotis. In Tamil Nadu, it is called *karamani* and the boiled beans are made into a dry snack called *sundal*. In Kerala, the beans are added to a pumpkin-based dish called *olan*, which is a part of the traditional *sadhya* meal. In Andhra cuisine, black-eyed peas are used to make a fried vada-like snack called *alasandalu*. In many Middle Eastern countries as well as Egypt in Africa, they are called *lobia*, a name that is used in many parts of India too.

Cowpeas come from a variety of yard-long beans, which are fairly easy to grow in the kitchen garden. If you get a good variety of seeds, they can turn into prolific producers. You can pluck the beans after they have matured and dried or turned a shade of light brown. Once you shell the dried beans, you have your very own homegrown black-eyed peas that can be stored for months. Beans like these restore nitrogen in the soil, giving a boost to any plant that is sowed in the next cycle.

There are a few different varieties of black-eyed peas available in India, which differ in size and colour (some have a darker brown shade). Their nutrient profiles are fairly the same so choose the ones that are easily available where you live.

Nutrition in black-eyed peas

One cup of cooked black-eyed peas provides 13 grams of protein, 11 grams of fibre, almost 90 per cent of the daily requirement of folic acid, and 25 per cent of the daily requirement of iron.

The protein level in these beans makes it a good choice for vegetarians and vegans. Protein along with soluble fibre makes it a useful addition to a diabetics' diet. Having a moderate GI of 42, it leads to a more gradual increase in blood sugar after a meal.

Black-eyed peas are a decent source of zinc, selenium and riboflavin. Zinc is an essential micronutrient for immune function, for most of the enzyme reactions in the body, and in protein production. Selenium is a powerful antioxidant that prevents inflammation, reduces the risk of some cancers, and is important for thyroid health, heart health, and immunity.

Adding black-eyed peas to the diet keeps the bowels regular as well. It also acts like a prebiotic, which provides nutrition to the good bacteria in the gut.

How to use

Unlike chickpeas and kidney beans, black-eyed peas need only three to four hours of soaking time. If using a pressure cooker or instant pot to cook them, the soaking time can be entirely done away with, but it is recommended.

1. Black-eyed peas add heft and extra nutrition to soups and salads.
2. Black-eyed peas are one of the best ingredients for meal prep. Keep a batch of cooked black-eyed peas in the refrigerator to add to salads, curries, soups, rice dishes, etc.

3. Cooked and mashed black-eyed peas can go into making vegan or vegetarian burgers.
4. Make curries out of black-eyed peas using recipes from different regions in India – Maharashtra, Mangalore, Punjab, Kerala – and you can never tire of it. Serve with rice or rotis.
5. Black-eyed peas pair well with onions, potatoes, tomatoes and spices such as bishop's weed (*ajwain*), cumin, ginger and asafoetida.
6. Mashed black-eyed peas can also be used as the secret ingredient to make healthy brownies.

BLACK PEPPER / PIPER NIGRUM

Black pepper, termed black gold, was used as currency in the Middle Ages. A study published in *Molecular Phylogenetics and Evolution*[8] explains how the spice came to India from South-East Asia more than five million years ago. This spice, which is intrinsic to almost every dining table today, has a fascinating history.

The spice routes were the earliest trade routes. Sailors braved treacherous sea voyages in search of precious goods, such as spices, to be traded. The price of pepper was extremely high in the Middle Ages and the trade was completely dominated by the Romans. In the mid-15th century, Portugal was the leading maritime nation in all of Europe. Under the leadership of Prince Henry the Navigator, all efforts were on to find a sea route to India to break the monopoly of the Romans, and to get a hold of the exotic spices from the East. The ruler at that time, King Manuel I, commissioned Vasco da Gama, the Portuguese explorer, to sail to India. Vasco da Gama became the first person to sail from Europe to India, taking the circuitous route around Africa, avoiding the caravan Silk Routes through the Middle East and Central

Asia. When da Vasco Gama arrived in Calicut, the existing Arab traders who were fluent in Arabic and Spanish asked him what had brought him there. 'Christians and spices,' he declared. His successful voyage was the start of 450 years of Portuguese colonialism in India.

The Portuguese dominated the spice trade for nearly a century only to be ousted by the Dutch, and around the beginning of 1635 by the British, who established pepper plantations.

Presently, Kerala, Karnataka, and Tamil Nadu are the top three pepper-producing states in India. Black pepper grows on flowering vines, which grow up to 10 metres in height, with the support of tall trees such as silver oak or supporting poles. The vines spread easily, wherever the shoots hit the ground. They bear fruit from the fourth or fifth year and continue for seven years thereafter. The fruits of the vine grow in a spike formation. Once the fruits at the base of the spikes start turning red, the spikes are harvested, allowed to dry and then the pepper fruits are stripped off the spikes to get black pepper. The premium Indian varieties of black pepper are Malabar Garbled and Tellicherry Extra Bold.

Nutrition in black pepper

The active compound in black pepper is piperine, which has antioxidant and anti-inflammatory properties. Animal studies have shown a connection between black pepper and improved blood sugar metabolism[9] and brain function.

Piperine also boosts the absorption of other vital nutrients. For example, the presence of black pepper improves absorption of calcium, selenium, and the nutritive compounds found in turmeric and green tea.

How to use

1. Although black pepper is available in powder form, it is ideal to grind whole peppercorns for use in salads, soups and pasta. Peppercorns can also be ground to a coarse or fine powder in a mortar.
2. Pepper *rasam* is a panacea for the south Indian soul, not unlike chicken soup in the West. Be it a cold or flu or an upset stomach, a light broth-like *rasam* with a kick from freshly ground black pepper is enough to put the spring back into our steps (or sinuses).
3. Pepper's mellow heat and bold flavour also makes it an important condiment in sauces and dressings, adding bags of flavour to dishes.

BROCCOLI / BRASSICA OLERACEA VAR. ITALICA

The neighbourhood supermarket stocking up hillocks of broccoli at ₹60 a kilogram in winters speaks for its growing

popularity – even though it is still labelled as an exotic vegetable in India. Although it was only used by high-end restaurants initially, broccoli has become more accessible in India and is regularly used by urban households and restaurants. It is one of the most popular vegetables used in 'continental' dishes.

Some people may have an inherent distaste for broccoli due to genetics. The gene TAS2R38 affects how we perceive bitter foods, and people with some variations of this gene are more likely to find broccoli unpleasant and bitter.

Nutrition in broccoli

Broccoli is low in carbohydrates and calories. It is rich in folic acid, a vitamin that is of utmost importance during pregnancy, and is also known to reduce the risk of cancers of the breast, colon, stomach and pancreas.

The presence of vitamins C, A and E makes broccoli an excellent choice for great skin health.

Broccoli also contains vitamin K, which is vital for the blood clotting process. Vitamin K also promotes bone health by improving calcium absorption and preventing calcium loss in the urine.

Like other members of the cruciferous vegetable family, broccoli has cancer-preventing properties. It is rich in the cancer-preventing antioxidant sulforaphane, which is especially effective in the cancers of the breast[10], colon and lung.

The carotenoids in broccoli are lutein and zeaxanthin, which are very good for eye health.

At just 31 calories for a cup of broccoli, it offers more than the daily required quantity of vitamin C and vitamin K, along with three grams of protein and two grams of fibre. This shows what a nutrition powerhouse this vegetable is.

As both cauliflower and broccoli belong to the same family, it is not uncommon to think of them as having a similar nutritional profile. While both are low in calories and carbohydrates and are high in fibre, broccoli has a higher concentration of vitamins A, C, E and K and calcium than cauliflower.

How to use

1. When buying, choose a tight head of broccoli with bright green florets. Turn it over and inspect under the stem for any soft, rotting spots. Yellow spots indicate that the broccoli has seen better days.
2. Like any other crucifers such as cabbage, cauliflower, etc., boiling is not the best way to cook broccoli. It gives out a sulphurous odour that is not very appetizing. The boiling method also leaches out the water-soluble vitamin C from the broccoli. Steaming it in a stovetop

steamer or in the microwave, sautéing it in a pan as a stir-fry, or roasting it in the oven are the most flattering ways to cook broccoli.

3. Steamed or roasted broccoli is great in salads when combined with apple, walnuts, and cheddar cheese.
4. Broccoli makes a good ingredient for soups in winter, as it is easily available in this season. Use it in combination with almonds, corn or peas.
5. Steamed broccoli florets tossed in garlic add a healthy serving of vegetables to cooked pasta.
6. A mixed vegetable stir-fry featuring broccoli, carrots, spring onions, spinach and zucchini makes for a colourful dish to go with rice or noodles.
7. To make it more appetizing for children, serve steamed broccoli florets with a cheese sauce and pasta.
8. Raw grated broccoli can be added to idli, dosa and *dhokla* batter to increase their nutritional content.

BUCKWHEAT / FAGOPYRUM ESCULENTUM

Buckwheat flour or *kuttu* ka atta is popular as an ingredient used to prepare dishes while fasting. All pseudo-grains and flours such as buckwheat, water chestnut flour, amaranth and its flour, samo rice, etc., are the preferred ingredients to prepare fasting dishes in north India as they are nutritious as well as filling in the absence of grains. Buckwheat flour is made into rotis, puris or pakoras for preparing food that is eaten during fasts.

Buckwheat is not related to wheat and is naturally gluten-free. It is common in China and Tibet, especially in mountainous areas where wheat does not grow. Soba noodles, which are made of buckwheat, are popular in Japanese cuisine. Roasted buckwheat is used to make tea in Korea, Japan, and China. I have also seen my friend

Michelle, who is of Korean origin, make the most addictive fried buckwheat noodles. Using just two ingredients, buckwheat and salt, and of course oil to deep fry, it makes for a most flavoursome snack. Buckwheat was introduced to France in the 12th century, where the flour is still used to prepare traditional crepes. Buckwheat pancakes, called blinis, are popular in Eastern Europe. Buckwheat spoon bread known as *adjovi žganci* is the national dish of Slovenia.

Bees love to feast on the rich nectar found in buckwheat flowers. The honey made by these bees is rich in flavour and dark in colour.

Nutrition in buckwheat

The colour of buckwheat is grey or light brown, much darker than wheat flour. This colour is from the hull that gets ground into the flour. Buckwheat is a quality source of protein, rich in the amino acids lysine, threonine and tryptophan. Soaking, sprouting and fermenting are ways to increase the bioavailability of nutrients in buckwheat. It is a good choice of carbohydrate for those who cannot eat wheat due to gluten sensitivity. Buckwheat is rich in minerals like iron, zinc and selenium, along with polyphenol antioxidants (like the tannins in tea) and flavonoids, particularly rutin. It is low to medium on the GI scale, making it good for diabetics as it causes a gradual increase in blood sugar levels after a meal. Buckwheat also contains quercetin[11], an anti-inflammatory antihistamine compound which fights allergic conditions.

A whole-grain carbohydrate rich in protein, fibre and minerals is a good choice for a healthy lifestyle. The fibre content keeps us full for longer as well. The high fibre content, low GI, and high satiety factor make buckwheat a healthy option for diabetics. Whole grains are known for their heart health benefits too. The magnesium in buckwheat relaxes blood vessels and is good for those with high blood pressure.

How to use

1. Soak the whole grain overnight and then allow to sprout for three days or so, by rinsing in fresh water and draining once a day. Soaking and sprouting reduces the anti-nutrients in buckwheat. Use these sprouted grains to prepare porridge, pulao, salads, *khichdi*, etc. It can also be used as an addition to soups.
2. Use the readily available flour to prepare *puris*. Add a portion of it to wheat flour to make *rotis* and *parathas*, or substitute 25 per cent of the flour content in baked goods, bread, crepes and pancakes with buckwheat flour.

Where to buy

Most local *kirana* (grocery) stores will stock buckwheat flour as it is regularly used for making dishes for fasts.

The whole grain can be found online or in health food stores and farmers' markets.

Buckwheat noodles (also called soba noodles) can be found in gourmet food stores.

CABBAGE / BRASSICA OLERACEA VAR. CAPITATA

Allow chopped cabbage and water to simmer in your kitchen—this is enough to set the most ardent cabbage fan on a run. The smell of boiling cabbage is possibly one of the vilest food smells. The sulphurous odours produced during boiling are due to the formation of a compound called trisulfides. There are a few ways to reduce the formation of this compound, such as cooking cabbage on a slow simmer versus a rolling boil. Adding vinegar, lemon or wine to make the cooking medium acidic also reduces the generation of this pungent odour.

One of the concerns to be addressed regarding cabbage is if people with hypothyroidism can consume it. Scientifically speaking, cabbage is one of the known goitrogens. What this means is that it has substances that inhibit the absorption of iodine by the thyroid gland. However, in order to have this effect, one must consume a rather large quantity of raw cabbage, which is unlikely to happen. Also, having enough iodine in the diet by way of iodized salt, potatoes, dairy products like yoghurt and paneer, chocolate, seaweed, etc., will more than make up for any impact of eating crucifers like cabbage. For someone who already has an underactive thyroid gland, and is on medication, i.e., external supplements of thyroid hormone, eating cabbage or any other goitrogenic vegetables like broccoli, cauliflower, kale or turnip, will not have any negative impact.

Nutrition in cabbage

Red cabbage is rich in anthocyanins that are found in the red-blue-purple family of fruits and vegetables. This antioxidant is known to enhance memory and offer cancer protection. Red cabbage has 10 times more vitamin A than green cabbage, and is higher in vitamins A and C, and iron levels. Red or purple cabbage adds a bright colour to salads, while it does turn into a dark grey when cooked as a *sabzi* or a dry curry. There is no reason to substitute green cabbage with red entirely. It is good to use the red or purple version to add more variety to a healthy diet and for the dose of anthocyanins that is available in the red-blue-purple family.

The cabbage soup diet *(No, I do not want you to try this!)*

This is a crazy, unsustainable diet for fast weight loss made popular on the internet. As an unverified backstory goes, this diet was designed by a hospital to make obese patients lose weight quickly before heart surgery. It involves eating only cabbage soup for a whole week with a few additions of fruit or skimmed milk. The possible upside of this diet is that it is easy to make a large pot of soup to cater for meals for two to three days. It is inexpensive. It does not need the dieter to go hungry as the recommended soup plus other permitted foods can be eaten as and when hungry. Weight loss does happen as a result of extremely low-calorie intake. But this diet is low on protein, leading to muscle loss, which is not good for weight management in the long run. The excessive fibre in the diet may cause bloating and gassiness in people not accustomed to a high-fibre diet. It is usually done for a week and if the dieter gets back to his/her usual high-calorie diet, the weight lost is bound to come back. The cabbage soup made along with a bunch of vegetables like bell peppers, onions, celery and mushrooms is a healthy one, and it can make a hearty dinner two to three times a week, as a part of a balanced diet and not by itself.

A cup of raw cabbage provides around two grams of fibre. This includes both insoluble and soluble fibre that prevents constipation, provides prebiotics to the beneficial bacteria in the gut and keeps cholesterol levels under control.

Antioxidants in cabbage protect the body from chronic inflammation.

Cabbage is an excellent source of vitamin C that is important for immunity and collagen production, the latter of which maintains the integrity of skin, bones and blood vessels.

The entire family of cruciferous vegetables have powerful anti-cancer properties[12] due to the presence of the sulphurous compound glucosinolates.

How to use

1. Sauté shredded cabbage in a pan to prepare a south Indian-style *thoran* or *poriyal*, with spices, tempering and coconut.
2. Tossed along with fresh peas (in winters) and cubed potatoes, cabbage makes a delectable dry curry to go with *rotis*.
3. Wedges of cabbage tossed in olive oil and salt, then oven-roasted until golden brown along the edges, can be used as a centrepiece for a salad.
4. Make coleslaw with grated cabbage and carrot mixed with hung yoghurt, grainy mustard, herbs and spices.
5. Try a Mauritian-style condiment called *achard legumes*, made using shredded cabbage and carrot – sometimes with the addition of green apple juliennes – tossed in curry powder and oil.
6. Use steamed cabbage leaves instead of lasagna sheets to make a low-calorie and low-carbohydrate lasagna.

Cabbage and fermentation

While cabbage by itself is loaded with health-boosting nutrients, in a fermented form, with the added goodness of probiotics, it is an almost unbeatable health food. Two of the most famous fermented foods in the world – sauerkraut and kimchi—use cabbage. In the process of fermentation, salt combined with shredded cabbage breaks down the natural sugars present in cabbage to produce lactic acid, which acts as a preservative.

The making of sauerkraut started off as a way to preserve a vegetable for the colder months or to carry on long voyages. Properly prepared and canned sauerkraut can last up to a year at room temperature, which was indeed a big deal in the days before refrigeration and before fresh produce was available all year round.

Kimchi is an iconic Korean dish that no Korean household will go without. This fermented cabbage condiment uses seasonings like red chilli powder, ginger, garlic and more, resulting in a complex flavour described as 'funky' and 'intensely umami'. The intense flavours of kimchi are also used in preparing dishes like fried rice and noodles. So integral is kimchi to Koreans that they even have a special kimchi refrigerator that keeps the fermented kimchi at an optimum temperature and helps retain its flavour for up to four months.

CARROT / DAUCUS CAROTA SUBSP. SATIVUS

Carrots get special love in India in the winters when the long red carrots make their annual appearance. In the northern states, black and purple varieties of carrots are also available during this season. A theory suggests that purple carrots originated in Afghanistan at the border of the Himalayan and Hindu Kush mountains. This variety was then domesticated in the neighbouring regions of India, Iran, Russia and Pakistan.

Carrot is one vegetable that straddles the savoury and sweet world with panache. If the baking world has its carrot cake, the Indian *mithai* world has its carrot *halwa*.

Carrot *halwa* made using seasonal red carrots is one of the culinary highlights of Indian winters. Raw, unprocessed sugar, vitamins and fibre from carrots, protein and calcium from milk and healthy fats from the nuts, all together make carrot halwa one of the more nutritious desserts. The elbow grease that one must put in to grate a kilo of carrots is a good pre-dessert arm workout.

If there is a savoury equivalent to the halwa, it must be *kanji*, typically made in north India using purple or black carrots. This drink – fermented using mustard seeds along with carrot batons and water – is full of probiotics, and the slightly tart carrot batons make an excellent snack by themselves or as an addition to salads.

Having grown carrots in my small kitchen garden, I can attest to the fact that it is quite a process. First, the feathery fronds shoot out in three to four weeks, growing bigger and bushier in the next couple of months. These carrot tops (leaves) have a dill-like flavour. I love snipping bits of these in the early stages to add to salads or to pesto. As the carrots grow beneath the soil, the leaves tend to get more mature and fibrous. Pulling out carrots from the ground three months after sowing is a hit or miss. Sometimes, you get a perfectly formed carrot, sometimes a tiny one that failed to grow, and at other times, a Halloween-esque malformed specimen.

Smaller varieties of carrots can be grown in a pot which is at least one foot deep. It is a gardening experiment worth engaging in, just for the joy of being able to pull out a carrot from the soil and using it in a dish. Growing your own carrots also gives access to the feathery carrot tops which are full of flavour, something which is very rare to find in a supermarket. Gardening supply stores and online stores sell grow bags which can be easily used for the purpose of growing carrots.

Nutrition in carrots

Around 100 grams of raw carrot (equivalent to one small carrot) is enough to provide 100 per cent of the daily required vitamin A. 'Beta carotene' gets its name from the word carrot, so it goes without saying that carrots are one of the richest sources of this nutrient. Carrots also contain other carotenoids such as alpha-carotene and lutein, both of which make it excellent for eye health. Lutein protects eyes from the harmful effect of UV rays.

Vitamin A in combination with vitamin C also protects the skin from UV rays.

Carrots convert their fatty acids to compounds called polyacetylenes that have shown anti-cancer properties against colorectal cancer and lymphocytic leukaemia[13] in lab and animal studies.

Carrots are a good source of biotin, a B complex vitamin that plays a role in blood sugar management as well as skin health.

The antioxidants and other micronutrients in carrots have a protective effect against cardiovascular disease, more so than other fruits and vegetables in the orange-yellow colour category. A large-scale study[14] from the Netherlands, in which participants were followed for 10 years, showed that people who ate a quarter cup more of carrots in a day had a reduced risk of cardiovascular disease compared to those who didn't.

How to use

The first question that needs answering is should carrots be peeled? Organic carrots can just be scrubbed and washed, used as it is. Others can be peeled lightly.

1. Carrots can be used in multiple ways in salads, giving a different visual appeal and texture depending on whether it is sliced, julienned, cut into batons, grated, spiralized or roasted. A combination with chopped walnuts, herbs and a grain (such as millet) makes for a delicious and hearty salad. Indian-style *koshimbir* (a type of salad) with grated coconut, peanuts, lemon juice and a tempering of green

chillies with mustard seeds is easy to make and a tasty addition to any meal. The addition of soaked and drained moong dal adds to the protein content.

2. Carrot sticks go well with hummus, peanut butter, or a hung curd dip. Cut the sticks and keep them in a jar of water in the fridge to prevent them from losing moisture and turning white on the outside.
3. Whole roasted carrots, Yotam Ottolenghi-style, topped with hung yoghurt, nuts, seeds and herbs is a delightful plant-based centrepiece for a dinner party.
4. Add grated carrots into *idli*/dosa batters, *upma*, pancakes, *poha*, etc., to get a hearty serving of this vegetable for breakfast.
5. Use carrots in soup in combination with lentils or herbs like coriander.
6. Grated carrots or carrot puree is a good ingredient to add to healthy bakes to reduce the fat content, and also to provide a natural sweetness, similar to applesauce.

CAULIFLOWER / BRASSICA OLERACEA VAR. BOTRYTIS

Gobi parathas, alu gobi, gobi matar – come winters in India and we cannot stop making these much-loved cauliflower dishes. This vegetable, which can translate into a variety of delicious dishes, is also powerfully healthy for us. So much so, that it has transcended the vegetable world and is now giving competition to one of the world's most popular grains, i.e. rice. The 'cauliflower rice movement', in which grated or finely processed cauliflower is used as a low-carb and low-calorie rice substitute is being sold in the rice/grain aisle in some supermarkets in the U.S., and many other countries in the world.

One should be careful while processing cauliflower. The spaces between the florets are home to green worms – small and large. Cleaning cauliflower thoroughly is very important to ensure that it is contaminant free before cooking it. Soak the florets in a big bowl of super salted water for 15 minutes to draw out the worms. Shake each floret, discard the water and wash again in fresh water. Dry thoroughly with a towel and proceed to use in cooking.

Boiling is not the best method to cook cauliflower as three minutes of boiling leads to significant loss of phytonutrients, which is comparable to 10 minutes of steaming.

Nutrition in cauliflower

Cauliflower is low in carbohydrates and calories, making it a very useful vegetable for weight watchers and diabetics alike.

Even though citrus fruits are thought of as the best vitamin C rich foods, cauliflower does not disappoint in the vitamin C department. A cup of cooked cauliflower provides nearly 75 per cent of the daily requirement of the immunity-boosting vitamin.

The phytochemicals in cauliflower provide antioxidant benefits and stimulate the immune system. They also reduce the mutations and multiplication of cancer cells, making cauliflower one of the best cancer-preventive foods. Cauliflower has been linked to a decreased risk of colorectal cancer when consumed regularly at least once a week. It also reduces the risk of prostate cancer and blood cholesterol. In fact, the entire cruciferous range of vegetables is known to reduce the risk of cardiovascular diseases[15].

One cup of cauliflower provides three grams of fibre, which is good for satiety, blood sugar, and cholesterol management, preventing constipation and working as a prebiotic in the large intestine.

How to use

1. Cauliflower florets can be steamed, pan-fried or sautéed in a variety of Indian curries, both dry and in gravy.

2. Oven-roasted cauliflower makes for a healthy snack or can be added to salads.
3. In winters, make chunky or smooth soups with cauliflower along with garlic, alone or in combination with other seasonal vegetables.
4. Combine with winter vegetables like red carrots and fresh green peas, along with lentils to make a Tamil-style *kootu*.
5. For more adventurous uses of cauliflower, use the grated vegetable to make rice dishes or pizza crusts.
6. Cauliflower florets dipped in a plain flour batter and deep-fried make an Indo-Chinese dish called *gobi manchurian*. It is tasty, but not the best way to reap its health benefits.

> Recently, popular TV chef Jamie Oliver was blasted for his 872 calories per serving cauliflower cheese pizza pie, which is like death by cauliflower.

CACAO / THEOBROMA CACAO

'Chocolate comes from cocoa, which comes from trees, which makes it a plant. Therefore, chocolate counts as a salad.' A lot of salad haters like to quote this line in good jest. The first part of this quote is very much true. The second part, however, is up for interpretation.

The journey from a cacao pod to a chocolate bar is long-winding and arduous. Each pod has a spongy white flesh in which there are many seeds or beans. These beans are fermented and roasted, after which they are ground to get cacao powder and cacao butter. Cacao powder is mixed with sweeteners to make chocolate bars. For chocolate to be considered a superfood, it needs to have at least 70 per cent cacao. The big difference between cacao and chocolate is that the former is a plant-derived ingredient and the latter is a highly processed food made in factories. Mass-produced chocolate is made by roasting and grinding the cacao beans. It is then mixed with sugar, milk powder, hydrogenated fats, other fillers, additives and preservatives, leaving it with no health benefits of the superfood it originates from.

Raw cacao beans, crushed into smaller pieces and lightly roasted, give rise to cacao nibs. Cacao nibs are the least processed way to eat chocolate and consuming them is the easiest way to get all of the health benefits associated with this superfood.

Theobroma cacao is a tree with stringent conditions for its growth and survival. It grows only within 20 degrees of the equator (Ivory Coast, Ghana, Indonesia, Brazil and Cameroon are some countries that fall in this belt), and in places below 1,000 feet in altitude. Apart from this, it needs shade, humidity, and a temperature that doesn't fall below 16 degrees Celsius. Eight countries produce 90 per cent of the world's cocoa. Cacao trees are not too amenable to farming. They are susceptible to a range of pests that can wipe off entire plantations in no time. When chocolate is used in its base form (and not as candy), it is in all reality a spice like cumin or cinnamon.

When it comes to chocolate, we must be conscious and choose from a 'fair trade' brand. This ensures that a fair price has been paid to the underprivileged farmers and that no child labour has been used in the harvesting and processing of cacao.

Nutrition in chocolate

Raw cacao powder has over 40 times the antioxidants found in blueberries. These antioxidants such as polyphenols, especially flavonols, cause relaxation of blood vessels, reduce inflammation, and improve cardiovascular health.

The compound theobromine present in cacao stimulates the brain and heart while relaxing muscles and dilating blood vessels, thereby reducing blood pressure[16].

The flavonoids in cacao improve both insulin secretion and insulin sensitivity, which is helpful for diabetics[17]. The antioxidant and anti-inflammatory effects of cacao help reduce the impact of chronic complications of diabetes. One must keep in mind that eating commercially available chocolate bars with a high percentage of sugar and a low percentage of cacao will not be beneficial to diabetics. On the contrary, it may worsen blood sugar management.

Cacao is rich in magnesium, which is important for heart health and glucose metabolism.

Cacao is very rich in iron as it is one of the best plant-based sources of this vital nutrient. Make sure to combine it with a vitamin C-rich food to ensure better absorption. Raw cacao is also an excellent source of calcium.

There is a reason why eating chocolate elevates the mood, leaving one feeling happier. The compounds in cacao trigger the secretion of neurotransmitters[18] such as serotonin, tryptophan, tyrosine and phenylethylamine, which are responsible for feel-good sensations.

How to use

1. A piece of dark chocolate is the perfect solution for when you're craving something sweet post-dinner.
2. A mug of hot chocolate, made by dissolving one or two pieces of dark chocolate spiced with a pinch of cinnamon, nutmeg or turmeric and mixed along with hot milk (dairy or your choice of plant-based milk) can be consumed as a nightcap.
3. Use raw cacao powder and cacao nibs to make raw brownies and truffles.

DARK GREEN LEAFY VEGETABLES

All edible plant leaves fall under the category of dark green leafy vegetables (DGLVs). Leafy greens are an endless source of health-boosting nutrients, available for free or very cheap, either growing as weeds that can be foraged, or sold by local vegetable vendors for a few rupees. DGLVs are very versatile and can be added to any of the existing dishes that you cook routinely.

Almost all the DGLVs, except for popular ones like spinach, come under the neglected and underutilized species. One of the reasons for this is the lack of awareness among people. Due to the combination of low awareness, low monetary value, and short shelf life, most species of green leafy vegetables are rarely found in shops or supermarkets.

The best place to find DGLV varieties is on pushcarts of street vendors or from those selling greens in the local markets. Often, street vendors and local grocers grow or forage the leafy greens and consume them as a part of their daily diet. The vendors are always happy to share their knowledge of local names for these greens and the ways to cook with them.

In India, each region has an astounding variety of DGLVs due to different climatic and soil conditions. It doesn't matter if you haven't heard their names or tried them before. Treat it like you would treat spinach and add it to any Indian or continental dish where leafy greens would find a place.

People might wonder why it's important to consume a wide spectrum of DGLVs when spinach is available. For one, it is good to expand the range of produce that we eat. It ensures sustainability rather than depending on a limited number of food crops. Many of these greens are not grown on a commercial scale, but by local farmers and villagers who could also benefit more with a growing demand. The shorter growing cycle of these greens helps the farmers make money while they wait for their main harvests. DGLVs have a common set of nutrients, but each one comes with its own micronutrients and health benefits. Enjoying a variety of these greens as a part of the daily diet ensures a steady supply of a wide range of nutrients. A lot of these DGLV varieties will not be available in the future unless efforts are made to consume them regularly and to raise awareness about their benefits among the masses.

Table 4.1: Commonly Used DGLVs With Their English Names

Local name	Commonly used in	Botanical name / English name
Arbi patta /Patra	West India / Karnataka	Colocasia leaves
Basale soppu / poi saag	Karnataka, Malabar region, West Bengal	Malabar spinach
Bathua	North India	Chenopodium album
Chakota soppu	Karnataka	Mountain spinach
Dantina soppu / Harive soppu / Chawli	South India, West India	Amaranth
Gongura	Andhra Pradesh, Telangana	Roselle
Haak	Kashmir	Collard greens
Keerai / Palak	Pan India	Spinach
Kusum bhaji	Chhattisgarh	Safflower leaves
Manathakkali Keerai / Kachi soppu	Tamil Nadu	Black nightshade
Mooli patta / mullangi keerai	Pan India	Radish greens

Local name	Commonly used in	Botanical name / English name
Mudakattan keerai	Tamil Nadu	Balloon vine
Ondelaga / Vallarai Keerai/ Gotu kola	Pan India	Brahmi
Poduthalai ilai	Tamil Nadu	Frog fruit leaf
Ponnanganni keerai	Tamil Nadu	Sessile joyweed
Sabsige soppu	Karnataka	Anethum graveolens / Dill
Sambar pasalai	Tamil Nadu	Water amaranth
Sarson / Sassive soppu	North India/ Karnataka	Mustard greens
Sirukeerai	Tamil Nadu	Amaranthus dubius
Sushni saag	Eastern India	Marsilea quadrifolia

Nutrition in DGLV

All DGLVs are low in calories and carbohydrates, high in fibre, and a low GI, having a negligible impact on blood glucose. It is therefore very useful for diabetics and weight watchers. The recommended intake for adults is between one to two cups per week, although there is no reason why these cannot be consumed more often in our daily meals.

DGLVs are rich in folate, a vitamin that is vital for heart health, and during pregnancy to prevent certain birth defects. A study also linked the consumption of folate-rich foods to a reduced risk of pancreatic cancer[19].

Leafy greens are also rich in vitamin C, which is important for immunity and collagen production.

In general, one cup of cooked DGLVs provides nine times the daily requirement of vitamin K. Vitamins A and K improve eyesight and blood clotting mechanisms. Fat-soluble carotenoids and vitamin K in DGLVs are best absorbed in the presence of fat. The tradition of adding freshly grated coconut to greens, prepared as a *poriyal* or *kootu* in south Indian cooking, ensures better absorption of these nutrients. Carotenoids are powerful antioxidants and they are said to prevent some types of cancers of the breast, stomach, skin and lungs.

DGLVs are rich in calcium but this calcium is not best absorbed by the body due to the fact that the DGLVs also contain oxalic acid that binds to the calcium. The leafy greens are a good source of non-heme iron. Iron deficiency leads to anaemia that manifests with symptoms of fatigue and dizziness. Eating DGLVs regularly can prevent anaemia.

Studies show that inorganic nitrate, a compound present in DGLVs, can reduce the build-up of fat in the liver in case of non-alcoholic fatty liver disease[20].

The cruciferous leafy greens such as collard, mustard, bok choy, radish greens, etc., have all the health benefits of cruciferous vegetables such as broccoli, cabbage and cauliflower.

In 2017, an engineer-turned-farmer, G. Sriram Prasad started Keerai Kadai to grow and supply over 100 indigenous varieties of greens and herbs in Coimbatore.

As of 2019, Keerai Kadai has over 25,000 customers across Coimbatore who buy these greens and herbs. Mr. Prasad's family have been into agriculture for many generations, but being in the field of Information Technology (IT) did not give him much exposure to farming. He quit his IT job to get into farming full-time, with the urge to do something useful for people and to give back to the society.

Out of a variety of 300–400 types of vegetables and fruits that he could grow, he decided to grow green leafy vegetables as they are easily affordable to everybody. 'There are 100+ varieties of leafy vegetables alone. We grow 125 types of greens in our own farm and we also share our seeds and collect produce from 135 contracted farmers in and around Coimbatore,' says Prasad. 'Our greens are grown with natural methods, but we do not claim to be organic as the groundwater could be contaminated with chemical fertilizers used by the surrounding farms.'

However, it is not easy to find seeds of all the native varieties of greens as they are becoming rarer. 'Initially, I had to explore 30–40 farms, find seeds and collect data over a two-year period. We started with 15 varieties in December 2017 and by mid-2019 we were growing 125 varieties,' shares Prasad about his journey as a greens farmer.

When asked about the time taken to harvest these greens, Prasad tells me that it takes roughly 25 days. The farmers can make more money as there are over 14 harvest cycles in a year as against three to five with other vegetables. The risk is much less. Even if one or two cycles are damaged by bad weather or pests, the farmers have the rest of the cycles to depend on for their livelihood.

Prasad is encouraged by the fact that the younger population is taking more interest in native varieties of greens and are ready to experiment with them. His initiative tells us that there is hope for these neglected and underutilized species as well as for the local farmers focused on growing them.

In Tamil Nadu, a lot of these green leafy vegetables are considered medicinal herbs and each one has a use for a particular condition or ailment such as hepatitis, fever, joint pains, etc.

Here are some of the DGLVs that are used in native medicine

- *Kasini* is useful for diabetics by regulating insulin level in the blood.
- *Mudakathan* is useful for treating arthritis/knee pain.
- *Ponnanganni* is good for the eyes and nervous system.
- *Ayyam panai* and *thuthi* are good piles remedies.

DATES / PHOENIX DACTYLIFERA

Dates are nature's own candy. Being one of the sweetest naturally occurring ingredients, it is an excellent substitute for processed sugar in many desserts.

Dates are available as dry, semi-dry and soft, in both seed and seedless varieties.

Although 75 per cent of dates is natural sugar, it still qualifies as a superfood as it has abundant minerals, vitamins, antioxidants and fibre.

Dates are the first foods that are eaten to break the fast each evening during the holy period of Ramzan, observed by many Muslims. A calorie and nutrient-rich natural food is logically the best thing to eat after a long fasting period.

In India, date puree and date liquid are also available, and both can be used to fortify dishes or used as a sugar substitute. A sweet date and tamarind chutney called *saunth* is a mandatory ingredient in chaat dishes such as *bhel puri* and *dahi puri* to add a sweet tanginess that balances the other flavours. It is also served as an accompaniment to snacks such as samosas.

Dates are one of the most popular foods in the Middle East. After all, its origin can be dated back to 4000 BCE in Mesopotamia, somewhere around present-day Iraq. Stuffed dates are a common item in Middle Eastern pastry shops, and are usually stuffed with almonds, cashews, cheese or a mix of powdered nuts. Dates are also added to savoury dishes to create a different flavour profile such as in the Moroccan tagine.

Nutrition in dates

Dates are rich in potassium, which is required for the proper functioning of the nervous system. Potassium also relaxes the blood vessels and keeps a check on blood pressure.

Phosphorus in combination with calcium supports good bone health, while selenium aids cell growth and repair and is also a powerful antioxidant.

Dates are also a popular vegetarian/vegan source of iron, which helps prevent and remedy anaemia.

Dates are an excellent source of fibre; 100 grams of dates provides 50–100 per cent of our daily fibre requirement, depending on the variety. With a very high proportion of insoluble fibre, dates help keep bowel movements regular and prevent constipation. One can eat three to four dates at bedtime to facilitate regular bowel movements.

Dates also contain a number of phenolic compounds that are potent antioxidants, which have antimicrobial[21] and anti-inflammatory properties[22].

How to use

1. Whole dates can be sliced and added to salads.
2. Prepare a porridge mix with ghee-roasted broken wheat (*dalia*), dried dates and almonds for a post-partum breakfast mix that is rich in iron and other micronutrients.

3. Add a couple of dates to smoothies and milkshakes.
4. Instead of sugar, use soft dates to make energy bars, *laddoos* and brownies.
5. Dates are a perfect sugar substitute for chocolate-based bakes as the colour blends in well.

FLAXSEED / LINUM USITATISSIMUM

My first exposure to flaxseeds was over a decade ago. I was trying to create eggless versions of some baking recipes on my food blog at the request of my readers. Some international blogs and websites had information about a 'flax egg' where flaxseed meal could be whisked with boiling hot water to create a foamy, beaten egg-like mixture. This worked well as an egg substitute. While not standing in for all the properties that egg brings to baking, it was a reasonably good substitute in tea cakes, muffins and brownies.

Flaxseed, also known as linseed, was primarily grown for its fibre, which was used in textiles. The scientific name of flaxseed is *linum usitatissimum,* in which *usitatissimum* means 'most useful' in Latin. The word linen has its origins in 'linum'.

Flaxseed is a winter crop. The major flaxseed growing states in India are Madhya Pradesh, Uttar Pradesh, Bihar, Chhattisgarh, Maharashtra, and Jharkhand. Flaxseed is called *alsi* in Hindi, Punjabi and Gujarati; *jawas/atasi* in Marathi, and *aalividhai* in Tamil.

Nutrition in flaxseeds

The two main beneficial components in flaxseeds are the high percentage of fibre and omega-3 fatty acids. Flaxseeds have both soluble and insoluble fibre which are good in preventing constipation, in blood sugar management, and in reducing low-density lipoprotein (LDL) cholesterol. It also acts as a prebiotic for the beneficial gut bacteria.

Flaxseeds are rich in protein, specifically the amino acids arginine and glutamine, which have a positive impact on heart health and immunity. Flaxseed is one of the best plant-based sources of dietary omega, making it very useful for vegans and vegetarians. The higher ratio of omega-3 to omega-6 is said to lower the risk of chronic ailments.

It is also a good source of magnesium and vitamin B1.

Flaxseeds are the best plant source of antioxidants called lignans. Lignans are said to reduce the blood glucose levels and fat in the body, thereby reducing the risk of metabolic syndrome. They are also an antioxidant. Lignans reduce the growth of hormone-linked cancers of the breast, uterus and prostate[23].

How to use

1. Whole flaxseeds can be pan-roasted until crunchy and used as a topping over salads, soups, oatmeal, etc. It can be used in combination with other seeds and nuts to get a good dose of a mix of healthy fats.
2. Flaxseeds can be roasted and ground with a mix of roasted lentils, chillies and other spices to make a south Indian-style *podi* that can be eaten with rice and ghee.
3. Flaxseeds can be ground to a meal and used to sneak in an omega-3 advantage, fibre and protein to a variety of flours to make breads, bakes, etc. Due to its high oil content, flaxseed meal can turn rancid in a few days on exposure to air. Storing it in an airtight container in the refrigerator prolongs its shelf life.
4. Flaxseed oil can be used along with any other cold-pressed oils in salad dressings.

GARLIC / ALLIUM SATIVUM

While communities in India such as Jains and certain Brahmin sects do not prefer to include garlic in their diets, a large section of the population of India uses garlic in savoury cooking and it is a part of the pantry essentials like potatoes, onions and tomatoes.

Garlic lends its unmistakable flavour to curries and dals, among other dishes. It is mostly used in combination with ginger as a ginger-garlic paste that is first fried in oil or ghee after which the other flavours are built into the curry base.

In my community, even though garlic is not traditionally used in cooking, its medicinal properties are harnessed in special post-partum meals. New mothers are served garlic *rasam* with rice as a simple lunch. This *rasam*, made with more than a handful of whole garlic cloves, is not for the faint-hearted. It is said to help with recovery after childbirth and with lactation too.

Italian cuisine also reveres garlic. A simple dish of *spaghetti aglio olio* uses just garlic, extra virgin olive oil and chilli flakes.

Garlic is said to have grown wild in ancient India but currently grows wild only in Kyrgyzstan, Tajikistan, Turkmenistan and Uzbekistan. As per details in farmingIndia.in, garlic is cultivated as a rabi crop from October to November in Andhra Pradesh, Bihar, Haryana, Uttar Pradesh, Odisha, Punjab, Uttarakhand, Rajasthan, Bengal, and other hilly regions. It is grown as both a rabi and kharif crop in India depending on the region, while in some states it is planted in both the rabi and kharif cycles.

Nutrition in garlic

When garlic is crushed, cut or chewed, sulphur compounds are formed. Most of the health benefits of eating garlic are attributed to these sulphur compounds. The active sulphur compounds in garlic are said to prevent mouth, oesophagus, and stomach cancers[24]. Sulphur is also important for maintaining cellular health, joints and connective tissue, and oxygen metabolism.

Garlic has antioxidant, antibacterial, and anti-inflammatory properties. It keeps blood vessels supple and reduces the likelihood of chronic inflammation that leads to plaque lining the vessel walls, i.e., atherosclerosis.

Around 20 grams of garlic eaten 1–2 times per week, which is around 10 small cloves of garlic, is the quantity required to be consumed to reap its health benefits.

The antioxidants in garlic also may prevent Alzheimer's disease and dementia.

Garlic works as a prebiotic just like onions, providing nutrition for good bacteria in the gut.

How to use

Use fresh garlic and not readymade pastes or powders to reap the maximum health benefits and flavour of garlic. Choose garlic with fleshy bulbs with flakes that are not collapsed or shrivelled. Garlic can be stored at room temperature in a cool dark place. Peeled cloves of garlic can be kept in an airtight container in the refrigerator for two to three days.

1. Sauté chopped garlic at a low temperature to prevent browning and burning and to preserve its health benefits. In Italian dishes, chopped garlic is added to olive oil even before heating the oil. Burnt garlic has a very unpleasant aroma and flavour.
2. Entire heads of garlic can be coated with olive oil and roasted in the oven to prepare a roasted garlic paste. This has an intense garlic flavour minus the pungency and has a natural sweetness. Roasted garlic paste can be added to dips, salad dressings, soups and lentils.
3. Garlic paste is used as a base in many curries, often in combination with ginger.
4. Garlic is a common feature in many Indian chutneys, in both raw and sautéed form.

5. Combining garlic with lemon juice, herbs and spices can cut down the need for salt in salads, potatoes, etc.
6. Rub raw garlic cloves over a toasted slice of a baguette before topping it with chopped tomatoes and basil.

GINGER / ZINGIBER OFFICINALE

Dried ginger is an all-important ingredient in *Deepavali lehiyam* (a spicy medicinal fudge), a part of Diwali mornings in some Tamil households. *Lehiyam* is a massive booster dose of all the digestive herbs consumed in anticipation of all the rich food that will be eaten over the next few days.

For me, there is nothing like ginger tea to lift the mood. I add either fresh ginger, powdered ginger or ginger oil to my tea, and sometimes all three. Dried ginger in powdered form is a good backup for when you run out of the fresh root.

The compound gingerol in fresh ginger is responsible for its characteristic aroma and pungency. Gingerols are related to capsaicins that are responsible for the heat in chillies. That is why adding a lot of ginger to a dish also increases the heat levels in the dish (i.e., makes it spicy).

In dried ginger, gingerols get concentrated making it more pungent, while cooking modifies the gingerols to give a less pungent flavour.

Nutrition in ginger

Ginger is indeed possibly the best digestive one can lay their hands on in an Indian kitchen. The active ingredient, gingerol, works well to combat nausea, indigestion, and even morning sickness in pregnancy. Eating ginger is said to reduce the gastric emptying time, thereby reducing any post-meal discomfort that some people experience.

Ginger has antioxidant and anti-inflammatory compounds. The anti-inflammatory properties appear to reduce muscle pain and post-exercise muscle soreness[25]. It has also shown some effectiveness in reducing menstrual pain when taken at the start of a period[26]. The anti-inflammatory effect is also beneficial in treating osteoarthritis and rheumatoid arthritis.

How to use

1. Fresh ginger has a very unpredictable shelf life in the fridge. The younger variety with more moisture content turns soggy within a few days in the fridge. If available, buy the drier variety of fresh ginger, scrub and wash well, and keep in a resealable bag in the freezer, where it will stay fresh for months.
2. Fresh ginger cut into juliennes and tossed in lemon juice is used as the main ingredient in a Burmese ginger salad called *gin thoke*.

3. To use in tea or curries, grate the frozen ginger on a fine grater. It has an almost wet powder-like consistency, blending well into salad dressings and any other dishes. Another useful hack is to use the edge of a teaspoon, not a peeler, to scrape the skin.
4. Ginger powder can be used for teas, salad dressings, and baked goods for a more consistent flavour. Do note that ginger powder is more concentrated. A quarter teaspoon of the powder is equal to one teaspoon of grated fresh ginger. Ginger extract is available in small bottles and comes with a dropper, which is great for making herbal infusions and adding extra flavour to ginger tea.

GREEN MOONG / GREEN GRAM (VIGNA RADIATA)

The book, *Agroecosystems of South India: Nutrient Dynamics, Ecology and Productivity*, written by K.R. Krishna covers the history of green moong in detail. To cite from this book, 'archaeological specimens of *Vigna radiata* from settlements on the banks of rivers, such as Krishna and Godavari, suggest that Neolithic people around the 2nd millennium used green gram regularly.' Green moong is mentioned in ancient Sanskrit texts, such as the Rigveda and Yajurveda from 5,000 BCE. The book also mentions how green moong cultivation was popular in the 18th and the 19th centuries among farmers in interior southern Karnataka and Tamil Nadu, where it was grown in rotation along with cereals. It was also the short duration crop of choice in north Karnataka and Andhra Pradesh. Growing green moong is profitable for farmers as it sells for a high price and also increases soil fertility for the next crop due to its nitrogen-fixing properties.

Ayurveda considers both, green gram and its split dal (moong dal), variety highly nutritious, easy to digest, and balancing to the *doshas*. Both moong dal and split green gram are used to make *khichdi* with rice. The flour made from whole green gram is also recommended as an exfoliating body scrub.

Nutrition in green moong beans

Moong beans are rich in vitamins, minerals, and enzymes. They are also a good source of potassium, iron, and fibre. A hearty source of folate, moong beans are highly recommended to be consumed during pregnancy. The sprouted beans contain fewer calories as compared to the unsprouted bean (by weight), and more free amino acids and antioxidants. Soaking and sprouting also make the nutrients more available to the body.

According to an article published in the *Journal of Chemistry Central*[27], moong beans have antioxidant, antimicrobial, anti-inflammatory, antidiabetic, antihypertensive, lipid metabolism accommodation, antihypertensive, and antitumor effects.'

Moong beans are also known to have antifungal and antimicrobial activity. This is especially useful against the H. pylori bacteria that causes stomach ulcers.

Green moong is rich in protein (one cup of cooked beans contains 14 grams of protein) and resistant starch, which make it an important addition to a diabetic diet. Resistant starch is a carbohydrate that reaches the large intestine intact without getting digested, where it ferments and acts as food for the good bacteria in the gut. It behaves like a soluble fibre giving the benefits of lower blood sugar levels, reducing the appetite, and making the cells more sensitive to insulin.

The potassium in green moong relaxes blood vessels, thereby causing a reduction in high blood pressure.

One cup of cooked moong beans has over 15 grams of fibre, which is nearly half the fibre requirement for the day. Compared to chickpeas and kidney beans, moong beans have more total dietary fibre and insoluble fibre. The combination of soluble and insoluble fibre makes it useful for digestive health, reducing cholesterol levels, and in acting as a good prebiotic.

How to use

Green moong is available as whole gram, split gram, split and skinned as yellow moong dal, moong sprouts, and as green moong flour. Be wary of using readymade sprouts raw due to possible contamination from the water used. The flour can be used to make *dosa* or *dhokla*.

1. Soak and cook whole green moong to prepare dal or curries.

2. Soak whole green moong along with other lentils and beans. Grind to make a batter which can be used as is or after fermenting, to make *dosa*-like preparations.
3. Cook soaked whole green moong and prepare a Tamil-style *sundal* with a tempering of red chillies, curry leaves, asafoetida, and a garnish of fresh coconut. The same can also be prepared in a sweet version by adding jaggery, coconut, and green cardamom powder.
4. Whole green moong makes a nutritious soup. Pressure cook soaked green moong with garlic, onion and tomatoes. Blend, simmer and season.
5. Use green moong sprouts in salads. The slight sweetness and crunch pairs well with apples, pomegranate and cucumbers. Sprouts can also be steamed lightly before being used in salads.
6. Green moong sprouts make chaat dishes like *bhel puri* and *pani puri* more wholesome.
7. Sauté moong sprouts, onions and tomatoes to make a dry curry to go with rotis.
8. Sprouts can be used to make a spicy Maharashtrian *misal* that goes with pav.

How to make moong sprouts at home

Wash one cup of whole green moong well and soak in a bowl of water overnight.

Drain and place in a muslin cloth. Tie loosely and keep it in a colander. Cover with a thick towel to keep up the temperature and humidity in the setup. The towel also keeps out the light, which results in longer sprouts. Sprinkle water on the muslin cloth twice a day to keep it moist but do not let it turn soggy. In 36 to 48 hours, the green moong will sprout. Once sprouted, remove and store in an airtight container in the fridge.

GREEN TEA

There are records of tea drinking in India as early as the 1st century BCE. Tea was grown in different parts of India but, driven by the British East India Company, its commercial production started only in the 19th century. World-renowned varieties of tea such as, Darjeeling and Assam, are from India.

Green tea is said to have its origins in China. There are interesting stories about its discovery by a herbalist Shen Nong. The story goes that the leaves from a nearby tea bush flew into the water he was boiling, resulting in a refreshing brew, and this was how tea was born. Archaeological research leads to the belief that tea cultivation and brewing began during the Hemudu culture, between 7,000 and 6,000 BCE.

In ancient times, green tea was the only way to drink the beverage. There was no processing of tea leaves involved.

The difference between green tea and black tea is that in the former, the leaves do not undergo the withering and oxidation process.

Steeping or brewing time is very important to make the right cup of green tea. Adding boiling hot water and allowing the tea bag or leaves to steep for too long results in a bitter brew. Typically, to brew green tea, the temperature of water used is between 61°C to 87°C as against the more processed tea (CTC) that is boiled in water to make the Indian-style chai. The more expensive varieties of green tea are brewed in cooler water for shorter durations, and the leaves can be reused to make almost three cups of tea.

If green tea is not to your liking, you can get similar health benefits from consuming green tea extract in the form of a capsule. The capsules may, however, have a high caffeine level, and an overdose of the extract may cause liver toxicity.

In Burma, tea is not just had as a beverage but also consumed in food. Fermented tea leaves are used in a salad called *laphet thoke*, which is extremely popular in Burmese cuisine. Tea leaves go through a string of processes and are then fermented for a period of four months to two years before they are sold.

Nutrition from green tea

Dr. William Li in his TED Talk, 'Can we eat to starve cancer,'[28] lists green tea as one of the anti-angiogenic foods to consume regularly to prevent cancer. These foods stop the growth of new blood vessels, therefore, starving the cancer cells. However, while lower cancer rates have been observed in countries where green tea is consumed regularly, it could well be an outcome of other lifestyle factors and not just green tea alone.

Regular consumption of green tea showed a modest reduction in total, as well as bad cholesterol (LDL). A study[29] published in the *Journal of the American Medical Association* in 2006 concluded that drinking green tea was associated with reduced mortality from all causes, including heart disease, but not with cancer.

While green tea advertisements regularly claim weight loss as one of the benefits gained by increasing the drinker's metabolism, this is rather insignificant. This only way this works is if sugary beverages like tea, coffee, and colas are replaced with zero-calorie green tea.

How to use

1. In winters, fill a flask with brewed green tea and sip it through the day instead of going for coffee with sugar and creamer or masala chai with sugar.
2. In summers, green tea can be had as iced tea with a squeeze of lemon and honey.
3. Green tea can also be brewed in water infused with herbs and spices such as lemongrass, mint, ginger or turmeric.

4. Add matcha to smoothies and juices. It can also be added to no-bake desserts such as truffles or raw brownies.
5. Matcha can also be added to salad dressings.
6. Sprinkle matcha powder over yoghurt bowls.

Matcha vs Green tea

Both matcha and green tea leaves are obtained from the Camellia Sinensis plant. The treatment prior to harvest is different for matcha. The bushes are covered to block out sunlight for 15 to 20 days prior to harvest. This increases their chlorophyll production, making the leaves turn a darker shade of green. There is more effort in the harvesting process for matcha as the stems and veins of the leaves are discarded and the leaf alone is used for the bright green powder.

Matcha is the tea used in Japanese tea ceremonies. It is often mixed with hot (but not boiling hot) water in a special heated bowl (*chawan*) with a bamboo whisk (*chasen*) to make a frothy mixture. To offset the bitter and grassy taste, milk or coconut milk is used in cafes. Matcha tea powder is also used for its superfood properties and vibrant green colour in smoothies and other beverages. As against tea, the entire leaf is powdered and consumed for making matcha, due to which it is much richer in antioxidants. This also gives it a higher content of caffeine as compared to green tea.

HEMP SEEDS

Hemp was primarily grown for its use in textiles. The durable material derived from hemp was used to make cloth, fibre, paper, and even canvas. Canvas made from hemp was strong and durable and was therefore used to make sails of ships.

Eventually, it was outlawed in most parts of the world and was replaced by cotton.

Since 2018, Uttarakhand is the first state in India to allow commercial cultivation of hemp. There are two varieties, Indica and Sativa. Indica has higher levels of tetrahydrocannabinol (THC), the active compound in marijuana, which is responsible for the mental effects. The Sativa strain has more of the cannabidiol (CBD) which is the active ingredient responsible for the therapeutic properties of marijuana.

Hemp is one of the most sustainable natural fibres. Hemp grows to 12 feet in 3–4 months, while cotton takes nearly nine months for full growth. One acre of land yields three times more fibre from hemp as compared to cotton, while using less water and improving the soil quality by fixing nitrogen. It is one of the most eco-friendly crops, with every part of the plant being useful.

Edible hemp is available as shelled, split or ground seeds and as hemp seed oil.

The hard outer shell can be removed using a mortar and pestle but it is a time-consuming process. Shelled hemp seeds are also called hemp hearts. They contain over 30 per cent fat so it is best to keep hemp seeds refrigerated or else they may turn rancid. The powder form can be added to smoothies. Hemp seed oil has a fragrant nutty aroma, and works as a great finishing oil over salads and pasta.

Given its controversial image, this raises the question of how safe it is to eat hemp. Does eating hemp seeds have any of the effects of cannabis? Can this be safely eaten by kids? Hemp seeds sold by health food brands are from the variety of Cannabis Sativa, which does not have psychoactive properties, so it is safe to eat. Hemp seed shells may contain trace amounts of THC (< 0.3 per cent). Thus, people who have been dependent on cannabis may want to avoid hemp seeds in any form.

In India, given that hemp is cultivated in Uttarakhand mainly, it is very much a part of the local cuisine. In Kumaoni cuisine, *bhang ki chutney* is made with the seeds, which is said to keep the body warm during winters.

Nutrition in hemp seeds

Hemp seeds are a very rich source of healthy fats with the best ratio of omega 3-6-9 fatty acids. One tablespoon of hemp seeds provides over 7,000 milligram of essential fatty acids.

Of the calories in hemp seeds, 25 per cent come from protein which has all the essential amino acids, making it a complete protein. Another 30 per cent of the calories are from fat, containing both omega 3 and omega 6 fatty acids. Omega 3 fatty acids are known to protect heart health and the combination of omega 3 and 6 in the right ratio fights inflammation.

Hemp is a rich source of vitamin E, which is a powerful antioxidant.

Hemp seeds are very rich in the amino acid arginine[30], which produces nitric oxide, a compound that keeps the blood vessels dilated. This, in turn, keeps the blood pressure under control and helps reduce the risk of heart disease. Intake of arginine has also been linked to reduced levels of C-reactive protein, which is a marker of inflammation in the body. This could be due to the presence of gamma-linolenic acid[31] (GLA) in hemp seeds.

The presence of GLA in hemp seeds reduces symptoms of premenstrual syndrome such as breast pain, irritability, and fluid retention. It also reduces menopausal symptoms.

Hemp seed oil when applied on the skin is good for skin repair and regeneration and also reduces inflammation. The oil when applied to the hair helps repair and condition it. Hemp seed oil when used in food is good for heart health and the immune system.

How to use

1. Hemp hearts are excellent as a topping over salads, soups, pancakes, bakes, bread, etc., adding a delicate nutty flavour.
2. Hemp seeds or hearts can be added to pesto and chutneys.
3. Part of the oil in salad dressings can be replaced by hemp seed oil. It can be drizzled over pasta or toasted bread.
4. Hemp powder can be added to smoothies.

MILLETS

The state of Karnataka has been at the forefront of the millet movement, taking steps to revive the cultivation and consumption of millets. Bengaluru has an annual Organics and Millets Trade Fair displaying millets of every variety, along with other organically grown produce from the state. There is also a large variety of ready-to-cook and ready-to-eat products made from millets.

How are millets different from staple grains like rice and wheat? Firstly, millets are a more sustainable crop that require less water. They grow easily in drought-prone areas. Rice needs nearly three times the water as compared to millets. In the future, climate change leading to hotter weather, lesser rainfall, and a shortage of water will make it difficult to grow water-intensive crops. Crops like millets will play a crucial role in providing food for the population.

In a way, our ancient food is also an ideal future food. Its shorter growing cycle suited the nomadic lifestyle when it was first domesticated. The shorter growing cycle helps present-day farmers to have a more productive land. Millets also stay for longer without spoilage.

In India, millets have been mentioned in some of the oldest Yajurveda texts, citing the foxtail millet (*priyangava*), barnyard millet (*aanara*) and black finger millet (*shyaamaka*), thus indicating that millet consumption was very common,

Millet names in some Indian languages

English	Sorghum	Pearl millet	Finger Millet	Little millet	Kodo	Foxtail	Barnyard	Proso
Hindi	Jowar	Bajra	Mandua	Kutki	Kodon	Kangni	Sanwa	Barre
Tamil	Cholam	Kambu	Kelvaragu	Samai	Varagu	Tinai	Kuthiraiwali	Panivaragu
Marathi	Jowari	Bajri	Nachni	Sava	Kodra	Kang	Shamul	Vari
Bengali	Juar	Bajra	Mandua	Kangni	Kodo	Kaon	Shamula	Cheena

Source: Published in *Millet Recipes – A Healthy Choice*, by the Department of Agriculture, Government of Karnataka, 2018

pre-dating to the Indian Bronze Age (4,500 BCE). Millets are currently grown all across India, with different geographical areas having a preference for different types of millets. Most of the world's commercial millet crops are cultivated in India, China, and Nigeria.

On our travels to Sikkim, I came across a local millet beer called *chaang*. Millet grains are fermented to make beer, which is served in a special silver and bamboo container with a bamboo straw.

Given the current popularity of millets as a health food, quite a few restaurants are coming up with a focus on millets in their menu. Some of these are – Prem's Grama Bhojanam in Chennai and Bengaluru, a restaurant serving only millet-based dishes; Vaathsalya Millet Cafe in Bengaluru, which serves dosa mix, malted drinks, millet thali and tiffin items; Bhoomika Millets restaurant in Bengaluru, which serves finger millet and dry fruit juice as well as a millet leaf *bajji*.

Nutrition in Millets

Different millets may have small variations in their nutritional profile, but are mostly similar.

Millets are a good source of compounds called plant lignans which, when eaten, are converted by the gut flora into mammalian lignans. These compounds are said to offer protection from breast cancer and other hormone-dependent cancers[32].

Foxtail millet has over 12 grams of protein per 100 grams as against 6.8 grams in rice. Barnyard millet has the highest fibre among millets at over 11 grams per 100 grams, as compared to less than one gram of fibre in rice. Little millet, foxtail and kodo also score well in fibre content. Being high in fibre, millets are a suitable addition to a diabetic's diet.

Pearl millet and barnyard millet are rich in iron, while finger millet is extremely rich in calcium.

All types of millets are rich in magnesium, which reduces the frequency of migraines, lowers high blood pressure, and decreases the risk of heart attacks. Millets are also a good source of copper, phosphorus and manganese.

Millets are a naturally gluten-free grain and the flour can be used in combination with other flours to use for gluten-free cooking.

How to use

1. Traditionally, finger millet (*ragi*) is always soaked, sprouted and then ground into a fine flour to make baby food.
2. Millets, like all other whole grains, benefit from soaking, to reduce the anti-nutrient levels. Soak for one to two hours. Drain and then cook the millets on a stovetop in a pan or in the pressure cooker or rice cooker. Soaked millets take about eight minutes to cook on the stove.
3. Millets can be used as a whole grain to make porridge for breakfast. It can be used as a rice substitute in south Indian cuisine and eaten with a variety of accompaniments. It can be used to make various flavoured rice dishes such as tamarind rice, lemon rice, coconut rice, etc.
4. A lot of Indian breakfast dishes such as *poha, upma, sabudana khichdi*, idli, dosa, etc., can be prepared using millets as the base.
5. Millets can also be cooked along with milk to make delicious *kheer*.
6. Millets can also be used in grain salads and to make heartier soups.
7. Given their mild flavour, they can be used in a variety of sweet and savoury dishes from around the world. In recipes that ask for quinoa, couscous or bulgur, any of the locally available millets can be substituted as they are neutral in flavour.

> **Millets and hypothyroidism**
> Millets contain polyphenols that impair iodine and thyroid metabolism. Iodine is essential for thyroid hormone production. Pearl millet especially might interfere with the optimum functioning of the thyroid gland even if there is no iodine deficiency. All other millets can be had in moderation. It is not recommended to eat millet as the staple grain or on an everyday basis if one suffers from hypothyroidism.

MORINGA LEAVES / MORINGA OLEIFERA

The *moringa* tree is more popular for the drumsticks that are used in Indian cuisine. It is easy to find this tree growing in the streets in many parts of India, with its feathery fronds and beautiful foliage. It is the shining example of a backyard superfood. Nearly every part of the tree such as the leaves, roots, seed, bark, fruit, flowers, and immature pods are either edible or have medicinal value. In 2008, the U.S. National Institute of Health named it 'the plant of the year' while recognizing that the *moringa* tree had the potential to reverse environmental issues while providing for our nutrition needs.

In all the time I stayed in Mumbai, I did not know of this tree or of its leaves, even though drumsticks were a regular feature in *sambar* at home. The first time I heard of the nutritive properties of the leaves was in medical college. Our professor of preventive and social medicine would praise *moringa* leaves at every given chance for being the poor man's superfood. This was way back in the late 1990s. Present times have seen *moringa* emerge as a superfood in the West with powder, tea, capsules and more such forms available. This has led to the inevitable ripple effect back home with people being more curious and accepting of *moringa* leaves as a superfood. We are lucky to have easy access to fresh leaves in many parts of India so we do not have to resort to the supplements or the powder.

The leaves are more fibrous and tougher to cook than spinach, which is in line with its higher fibre content. My grand-aunt, who has been cooking and eating drumstick leaves all her adult life, has a tip to ensure better cooking of these leaves. Adding a pinch of baking soda to the chopped leaves along with water and pressure cooking it breaks down the fibres in the leaves, ensuring better cooking and digestion too.

One state which does full justice to moringa leaves (called *sajana saga* in Odia) in its cuisine is Odisha. *Moringa* leaves in combination with moong dal is a popular way to prepare these greens.

The flowers of the moringa tree are also edible. It is made into *pakoras*, or prepared as a *thoran* or in combination with peas. The flowers attract bees due to their nectar. *Moringa* oil is added to soaps, oils and other cosmetic aids for its anti-ageing, anti-wrinkle properties.

NUTRITION IN MORINGA LEAVES

According to a paper from the *International Journal of Phytotherapy Research*[33], 'gram-for-gram comparisons of M. oleifera leaves (fresh and dried) and other common nutritional plant sources reveals that M. oleifera provides more than seven times the vitamin C found in oranges, 10 times the vitamin A found in carrots, 17 times the calcium found in milk, nine times the protein found in yoghurt, 15 times the potassium found in bananas and 25 times the iron found in spinach'.

Apart from this, the leaves are also a good source of phosphorous, copper, folate, pyridoxine, beta carotene, and essential amino acids which are essential metals, vitamins, powerful antioxidants and building blocks contributing to immunity, several vital enzyme reactions, and bone and dental health.

Moringa leaves are rich in the antioxidants quercetin and chlorogenic acid, which reduce inflammation and prevent cancer. *Moringa's* anti-cancer effect comes from its property of preventing the growth of cancer cells.

Moringa leaves display anti-diabetic properties in both type 1 and 2 diabetes.

How to use

1. Use finely chopped leaves to a mixed lentil batter or a rice batter to prepare *murunga elai adai*. These can also be added to dosa batter to prepare *uthappam*.
2. *Moringa* leaves can be added to *sambar* or dal.
3. They can be prepared into a Tamil-style *poriyal*, Kerala-style *thoran* or an Odisa-style sabzi with moong dal.
4. *Moringa* leaves can be brewed with ginger to make a herbal tea.

MUSHROOMS

Mushrooms belong neither to the plant nor the vegetable category, but the fungi category.

While plants convert sunlight into food, mushrooms thrive in dark and damp places, deriving their nutrition from rotting vegetation found on tree barks, damp grass, and forest floors.

There are nearly 70,000 varieties of mushrooms, but only a handful of popular ones are used in cooking. Some of the well-known edible varieties are button mushrooms, oyster mushrooms, cremini, portobello, enoki and shitake. In India, button mushrooms are commonly available in most supermarkets. The other common variety is oyster mushrooms (pleurotus ostreatus).

Recently, another type of mushroom is being stocked in supermarkets and it goes by the name of 'milky mushrooms'[34] (calocybe indica). These have a bright, all-white colour and thick cylindrical stems. Being a warm-weather-loving species with a long shelf life of five to seven days makes it popular among mushroom cultivators in India. It was originally described in 1974 by botanists R.P. Purkayastha and Aindrila Chandra in West Bengal, after noting its popularity in the local markets. This is the first Indian mushroom variety to be commercialized by the Indian Institute of Horticultural Research in Hesaraghatta, Bengaluru. It is increasingly being cultivated in south Indian states all year round due to its preference for warm and humid weather conditions. Fast-growing, long shelf life and nutrient-rich – these are some of the properties that make milky mushrooms not just economically viable but also a sustainable way of food production to address world food demands. It is also an environmentally friendly way to produce a protein-rich alternative to meat. These mushrooms are rich in zinc and vitamin E.

Dried mushrooms are sold in South-East Asian countries. Consider buying these on your travels to these parts, as they last for many months. These are reconstituted in hot water and then used in dishes. Even the water is rich in mushroom flavour and it can be used as a stock.

Note: Do not experiment with foraged mushrooms as they could be poisonous.

Nutrition in mushrooms

Mushrooms have been used in Chinese medicine since ancient times for their health-boosting properties. A cup of whole raw mushrooms (approximately 100 grams) is just 21 calories. Mushrooms are low in carbohydrates with three grams of protein and nearly two grams of fibre. They are a good choice for a low-carb, high-protein meal for vegans and vegetarians. Given the protein and fibre content, it is a very useful addition to a diabetic diet, as well as those aiming for weight loss.

Mushrooms are rich in B vitamins like niacin, pantothenic acid and riboflavin, along with essential minerals like iron. B vitamins play an important role in converting the food we eat into energy and in the formation of red blood cells.

In the case of mushrooms, cooking releases more available nutrients and deactivates trace levels of a compound called agaritine present in the mushroom[35], which is said to be carcinogenic in very high doses.

Mushrooms are rich in antioxidants like selenium, vitamin C, and choline. They also contain another powerful antioxidant called ergothioneine, which has anti-inflammatory properties. Due to the thicker cell walls in mushrooms, this compound gets released upon cooking, which is another reason to consume mushrooms in the cooked form.

How to use

While choosing mushrooms, buy those which have stalks tightly attached to the caps. This indicates that the mushroom is fresh. The older the mushrooms, the wider the gap. The surface should not be bruised or slimy. Mushrooms when soaked in water behave like sponges. While cleaning them, keep water exposure to a minimum. The best technique to clean mushrooms is to wipe each one clean with a wet cloth. Another acceptable way to clean mushrooms is to use a small brush and dust each mushroom of any grit. This is, of course, a time-consuming method.

1. The easiest way to use mushrooms is to halve them and sauté in olive oil. Remember never to salt the mushroom while sautéing as it will end up drawing out all the water

out of the mushrooms. The mushrooms will end up boiling in water instead of getting sautéed and golden brown.

2. Finely chopped and sautéed mushrooms can be added to a pasta sauce or to an omelette.
3. Sautéed mushrooms make for a hearty filling in a sandwich or as a topping for bruschetta.
4. Indian-style curries can be made with mushrooms in combination with fresh peas, capsicum, spinach or *methi* leaves.

What is mushroom coffee?

Instant coffee mixed with mushroom powder (picked, dried and ground mushrooms) gives a black coffee an earthy and rich flavour, and not so much a mushroom flavour. It usually has half the caffeine content of a regular coffee. Mushroom coffees tend to have a mix of maitake and chaga mushrooms, to harness their antioxidants, blood sugar regulators and anti-cancer agents.

NUTS

Nuts are one of the few foods that are not only good for us but are also addictively tasty. Most people I know cannot stop at a handful. However, when it comes to nuts, portion control is important.

Peanuts, cashews, almonds, walnuts, and pistachios are some of the most commonly available nuts in India. While hazelnuts, Brazil nuts, pine nuts, macadamia nuts, pecans are also available these days, they are mostly imported, which makes them fairly expensive.

To roast or not to roast

All nuts taste better when roasted. Roasting deepens the flavour of nuts, making them tastier. Nuts can be roasted in the oven on a baking tray at a low temperature (up to 75°C) or on a stovetop in a heavy-bottomed pan. You can also roast nuts in the microwave by spreading it out on a glass baking pan and microwaving for two minutes or so. While using nuts in baked goods, the nuts need not be toasted but doing so makes them retain a better crunch in the finished product and also gives a more pronounced flavour.

Different nuts react differently to roasting. As a rule, keeping the temperature low and roasting for a short time will cause minimal nutrient damage. Contrary to popular belief, roasting reduces shelf life so roast smaller quantities that can be used within a week. The best practice is to buy raw nuts and roast them at home as per your requirement as store-bought roasted nuts may use additional oil to roast as well as added salt and sugar, all of which are avoidable when nuts are being added to the diet for their health benefits.

Salted vs. unsalted nuts

Most nuts are naturally low in sodium and rich in magnesium and potassium, which makes it a heart-healthy food. Therefore it does not make sense to negate the heart-healthy benefits by increasing the sodium consumption via salted nuts.

All nuts are low GI foods and can be consumed by diabetics for their health benefits. Nuts are rich in monounsaturated fats and the powerful antioxidant vitamin E, all of which have a protective effect on the heart.

Table 4.3: Common Nuts with Highlights and Health Benefits

Peanuts	• Technically a legume, but treated as a nut due to usage • Highest protein content among all nuts at 40 grams a cup • Used extensively in Indian cuisine • Most eaten nut butter • Rich in phenolic antioxidant resveratrol (similar to red wine)
Cashews	• Came to India via Portuguese explorers and to this day, Goa is a big producer of cashews • Great in stir-fries, salads and as a garnish in Indian sweet dishes • Can be used to make nut milk • Rich in copper, phosphorus, zinc
Walnuts	• Walnut cultivation in Kashmir is said to have its origins in Persia • Available with the hard shell, as whole shelled nuts and as halves • Seven walnuts are enough to provide the entire omega-3 requirement for the day • Rich in antioxidants, anti-inflammatory compounds, phenolic compounds (mainly from the skin), and vitamin E • Used very commonly in baking and in salads in American cuisine

Almonds	• One of the lower calorie nuts • Highest content of polyunsaturated fats • Rich in biotin and vitamin E • Its skin is rich in antioxidant flavonoids, so it is best consumed with skin • Used in Indian desserts like *burfi, kheer,* etc., and as a garnish for sweets • Used in baking recipes as a nut and as a flour substitute in flourless cakes • Its flour is also gluten-free
Pistachios	• Origins in Central Asia and the Middle East • Sold with and without shell, salted and unsalted • Main ingredient in many Middle Eastern desserts • Often combined with saffron and used in many Indian desserts • A serving of 30 grams of pistachio has 3 grams of fibre and 6 grams of protein. • One of the best vegetarian sources of vitamin B6 (pyridoxine)
Pine nuts	• Known in India as *chilgoza*; it grows in the western Himalayan forests in some parts of Kashmir and Himachal Pradesh • They are the edible seeds from pinecones • Unique grassy or piney flavour • Rich in vitamin E, manganese, phosphorus, zinc, and iron • An essential ingredient in the Italian pesto

Hazelnuts	• Turkey is the largest producer • It can be eaten raw, roasted, or as a paste • Used in Nutella and Frangelico liqueur • Very rich in manganese (reduces oxidative damage) and a good source of vitamin E
Pecans	• Mainly used in southern American bakes like pies and cakes • Very rich in antioxidants from flavonoids • Richest source of gamma-tocopherol form of vitamin E among all nuts, which is a powerful antioxidant that prevents cholesterol oxidation and reduces atherosclerosis
Macadamia nuts	• Native to Australia • Compared to other nuts, these are higher in fats and lower in protein, which lends to its buttery, creamy texture, and flavour. • Higher flavonoid levels as compared to other tree nuts • Good source of thiamine and manganese • Used in bakes, desserts, ice creams, etc.
Brazil nuts	• Origins in the Amazon rainforest • Large sized nuts; a serving of just three nuts = 100 calories • Just one Brazil nut provides the daily requirement of selenium, an essential mineral for thyroid function, immunity and cell growth (to avoid selenium overdose, do not exceed intake of over one to three nuts per day).

How to use

1. Add a tablespoon of chopped nuts to breakfast oatmeal or porridge.
2. A mix of nuts can be chopped and toasted along with other ingredients for a homemade granola mix or baked into granola bars.
3. Prepare a homemade trail mix with a variety of nuts, dried fruits and seeds to carry on journeys, runs and treks as a healthy source of high energy. It also makes for a good pre-sport snack for kids.
4. Use lightly toasted nuts along with green herbs (like basil) and extra virgin olive oil to make pesto, which can be used in a sandwich, salad or in pasta.
5. Add chopped nuts to muffin and cake batter and sprinkle nuts over the top too.
6. Garnish Indian breakfasts like idli, *upma, poha,* etc., with nuts like cashews and peanuts.
7. Peanuts and cashews make a great addition to Indian and South-East Asian salads. Sprinkle toasted and chopped nuts over individual portions of salads so they retain their crunch.
8. A garnish of cashews, lightly fried in ghee, adds a lot of flavour and interest to all Indian rice-based dishes like coconut rice, *bisibele bath*, pulao, etc.
9. Dip larger nuts like walnuts and pecans in melted dark chocolate to make a simple and healthy dessert.
10. Chopped pistachios or cashews make a good garnish for Indian desserts like *halwas* and *burfis*.

ONION / ALLIUM CEPA

In China, onions were grown as early as 5,000 years ago. In India, Charaka Samhita, the text on Indian traditional medicine from 400–200 BCE, mentions the properties of onions as a diuretic and digestive, and also deems it good for the heart, the eyes, and the joints. Chinese traveller Hiuen Tsang, during his visits to India in the 7th century, noted that very few people ate onions and those who did were 'expelled beyond the walls of the town'. It was in the 16th century that the Mughals popularized the use of onions in cooking. Certain vegetarian sects including Jains and some Brahmins do not consume onions even today.

Onion is probably the one ingredient that adds the most flavour to Indian food. There is no debate on whether onions are good for health. These are one of the cheapest foods to stock up on and eat in various forms to enjoy a variety of health benefits.

Several varieties of onions are available in India – the most common ones being the red, white and yellow varieties. In the rural parts of India, a smashed onion and green chilli is often an accompaniment to a thick millet-based roti that farmers carry to their fields for lunch.

Onion powder is available in many supermarkets, to add the flavour of onion to dry masalas and curries. The Indian supermarkets in the US never fail to stock up on bags of deep-fried and dehydrated onions, which are the quickest way to add flavour to any curry, and of course to a biryani.

Nutrition in onion

Onions are low in calories but concentrated with nutrients like vitamins, minerals and fibre. Onions are rich in vitamin C, which helps build better immunity, aids in collagen production, in the healing of wounds, and in protection from free radical damage.

They are a good source of potassium, which is important for muscle and nerve function, and keeps blood vessels relaxed, thereby preventing high blood pressure. They are also responsible for fluid balance in the body.

Onions contain a mix of over 50 sulphur-rich compounds. One of them is allyl sulphide, which has anti-cancer properties.

Onions are also rich in the antioxidant quercetin[36]. This compound is said to be a powerful antibacterial. It also fights free radicals, thereby preventing inflammation, certain cancers, fighting allergic conditions, reducing blood pressure and the risk of heart disease. Red onions are rich in the antioxidant anthocyanins which are said to reduce the risk of heart disease.

Consumption of onions leads to the production of glutathione that acts as a liver antioxidant.

Onions are also rich in calcium and folic acid. The chromium in onion helps cells respond to insulin and is therefore useful for diabetics. Being a good source of fibre, onion is also a good prebiotic, feeding the good bacteria in the gut.

Some of the sulphur compounds of onions are more active in the raw state and some others in the cooked state. It is good to consume a mix of raw and cooked onions in one's everyday diet.

How to use

Preparation

The best way to prepare onions or any other vegetables of the allium family for optimum health benefits is to chop them and let them sit for 5–10 minutes before cooking. This gives time for enough synthesis of the sulphur compound thiopropanal sulfoxide (the compound responsible for tears) in the onions. This compound is responsible for most of the onion's health-boosting properties.

However, how to chop onions without breaking into tears is every home cook's eternal dilemma. There are two tried and tested methods. One is soaking onion halves in a bowl of water for 15 minutes before wiping them dry and chopping them. The other one is a slightly more dramatic option, which is to wear goggles/glasses to prevent the onion fumes from hitting the eyes. Or else, there is always the food processor.

How to use

1. Raw sliced onions along with green chillies are often served as an accompaniment to an Indian meal (mostly north Indian). This crisp and pungent accompaniment clears the sinuses and gets the salivary glands going.
2. Pickled onions are also served along with a north Indian meal. Small-sized onions are soaked in vinegar for a length of time. This adds a nice tart flavour while dialling down the eye-watering pungency of the onions. Sliced onions marinated in vinegar is also an excellent way to add onions to salads, minus the pungent bite. Slice and soak onions for at least 30 minutes in a mix of white vinegar and salt. Squeeze well and add to salads.
3. Being versatile, chopped onions can be added to literally every savoury dish in Indian cuisine, from breakfast to snacks, to main course dishes like curries, rice, dal, parathas and so on.
4. Sautéed onions are a standard fixture in many Indian curries. In fact, if you cannot make up your mind on what to cook, you can start by sautéing onions and use that time to make your decision. Proper sautéing takes around 10 minutes for the onions to soften and lose their raw taste.

5. Properly caramelized onions take around one hour on low heat to get the golden brown colour and jammy flavour, minus any of the cheat steps like adding sugar or soya sauce. Caramelized onions, figs and goat cheese make one of the best flatbread or pizza toppings.
6. Deep-fried onions called *birista* are used to add flavour to biryani. These are available in some stores.
7. Onion powder is also available these days. It is an excellent addition to prepare dry masala mixes and to add onion flavour to curries without the hassle of chopping onions.

PINEAPPLE / ANANAS COMOSUS

Christopher Columbus came across a fruit that looked like a large pinecone with an interior texture resembling apples and he went on to name it 'pineapple'. This is another valuable commodity that originated in South America and was introduced by Spanish and Portuguese explorers to their colonies in the 16th century. If you get past the rather intimidating exterior, the pineapple is a rather fine fruit to know. Whether it deserves to be a pizza topping is a much-debated topic on the internet, but there is no debate over the fact that pineapple is a fruit stuffed with nutrients.

Pineapple with its sweet and sour taste, refreshing juiciness and flesh that holds its shape can be eaten raw or cooked in both sweet and savoury dishes. South Indian cuisine showcases the fruit in a variety of curries such as *gojju* from Karnataka, *pachadi* from Kerala, and *rasam* from Tamil Nadu. Pineapple cubes in *raita* are sublime when paired with a spicy rice dish.

The leftover crown of the pineapple can be sowed in the soil, which will grow into a pineapple plant, retaining all the properties of the original fruit.

The eyes on the surface of the pineapple are not some haphazard arrangement. In the 1820s it was learnt that the positioning of the eyes on the fruit follows curving rows and are set to a precise mathematical equation called the Fibonacci series.

Nutrition in pineapple

Pineapples are rich in vitamins A, C, and E, making it good for skin and eye health. Both vitamins C and E are powerful antioxidants that prevent oxidative damage in tissues throughout the body. Vitamin C is important for the production of collagen and the neurotransmitter serotonin. Our mood and sleep-wake cycles are influenced by this chemical.

Vitamins B1 and B6 in pineapples help boost metabolism, as they are a part of innumerable reactions in the body.

Pineapple is also rich in the mineral manganese that contributes to strong bones and connective tissue. This, along with the anti-inflammatory effect, makes it a very useful addition to the diet of those with arthritis.

Bromelain is a protein-digesting enzyme present in pineapple. This is the reason many people experience a range of reactions when they eat a pineapple, such as a mild throat itch to full-blown allergies. Due to its protein-digesting capacity, bromelain also breaks down mucus and helps in conditions of cough and asthma. Those with regular respiratory allergies should make pineapple a part of their diet, as it helps keep mucus thin and reduces the symptoms of allergies. Bromelain's anti-inflammatory, blood thinning, and anti-cancer properties are being studied at present.

How to use

Pineapple has a slightly different composition compared to other fruits — it does not have any starch reserves of its own. The 15 per cent sugar content in the fruit needs to be present before harvesting because it has no potential to ripen after it's harvested. Unlike bananas and mangoes, pineapples need to be harvested when they are fully ripe. While buying, the best guide to pick a perfectly ripe fruit is to smell it. A sweet, rich aroma indicates ripeness, as do the green leaves on the top of the fruit. Take care that there are no soft or dark spots on the fruit or an overripe smell, which may indicate that the pineapple is past its prime.

It is understandable to get deterred by a pineapple's intimidating looks. Given its rough, thorny and thick skin, a sharp and sturdy knife is needed to prepare the fruit. Remember to wash the fruit before cutting through it so all the surface microbes and dirt do not seep into the fruit. The best way to start is to chop off the leafy end and the bottom until you get a stable, flat surface at both ends. Place it on the chopping board and run the knife down the sides until the skin comes off and the flesh is exposed. With the pointy end of the knife, scoop out any leftover eyes on the fruit. After this, the pineapple can either be sliced or diced.

These days many supermarkets have counters that will cut the fruit for free. If done hygienically, this is a good option. For baking and dessert needs, or for a more consistent flavour as well as a convenience through the year, you can use fruit canned in water and not in sugar syrup.

How to use

1. There's nothing more refreshing than a perfectly ripe pineapple seasoned with a pinch of salt and red chilli powder.
2. Cubes of pineapple add natural sweetness and juiciness to a salad. Use pineapple in a grain salad and the grains will absorb the released juices and flavours when left to sit for a couple of hours in the refrigerator.

3. It can be the star of a vegetarian barbeque. Skewer chunks of pineapple with other vegetables and paneer. Coat with a marinade and grill until slightly charred around the edges.
4. Harness the fresh flavour of pineapple to make mouth-watering chutneys, both raw and cooked. Pineapple salsas are very popular.
5. Pineapple *gojju*, a sweet-sour-spicy curry from Karnataka, is a must-try, and is eaten along with steamed rice.

POMEGRANATE / PUNICA GRANATUM

It is indeed a gift that we have some foods that are both super healthy and also incredibly delicious. Sweet, juicy and mildly tart, what's not to love about pomegranates? Each seed (also called aril) bursts to release the most refreshing juice, which is a sheer eating pleasure for something that is so full of nutrients.

The fruit is native to the belt between Iran and north India. India is the largest producer of pomegranates in the world, followed by Iran. Pomegranate juice is boiled down until thick and the resulting molasses is used to prepare a famous Persian dish called *fesenjan* stew. Before the arrival of tomatoes to this part of the world, pomegranate juice, seeds and molasses were used to add sourness to Persian dishes.

Most Tamil wedding feasts serving curd rice will either have pomegranate or grapes as a garnish and Tamil folk can be very opinionated on whether pomegranate belongs in curd rice. I quite like biting into these tasty morsels, which provide bursts of relief from the bland curd rice. Pomegranate is also one of my favourite ingredients to add to a salad.

Birds and squirrels seem to have an affinity to this fruit. I realized this when for three years in a row, all that was left in the pomegranate tree in my garden was hollowed out fruit shells. The predators are experts at eating all of the delicious fruit via a small hole poked into the fruit.

Dried pomegranate seeds called *anardana* are used in chutneys and curries in north Indian and Pakistani cuisine. Dried seeds are also ground and used as a spice powder. *Anardana* is the main souring agent in *pindi chhole*, a chickpeas dish from the North-West Frontier Province. A piece of pomegranate peel is also added to the chickpeas during the cooking process to give the dish a darker colour.

It is a matter of convenience that both shelled pomegranate and the juice are easily available in supermarkets these days. The disadvantage of buying pre-shelled fruit is that it tends to become soggy in a couple of days in the fridge, losing its crunch and fresh flavour. Even brands that claim to sell 100 per cent pomegranate juice often spike their product with corn syrup, so make sure you check the list of ingredients on the pack.

Nutrition in pomegranate

Pomegranate is rich in vitamin C, the antioxidant that plays an important role in immunity and skin health among others.

Pure pomegranate juice is said to have more antioxidants than red wine. Polyphenolic antioxidants (anthocyanins and ellagitannins) in pomegranate, responsible for its vibrant colour, have anti-inflammatory properties that lower the incidence of atherosclerosis (plaque deposits) in blood vessels. Pomegranate juice has also shown to reduce blood pressure[37] both in the short and long term. The antioxidants in pomegranate are also seen to be helpful in arthritis by reducing inflammation.

Pomegranate has compounds with anti-angiogenic properties which can stop the growth of cancer cells. Studies are on to show the effect of pomegranate products in slowing the growth of prostate cancer[38].

The presence of a compound called punicalagin helps preserve skin collagen and slow down the signs of ageing.

How to use

Shelling a pomegranate is a bit tiresome. There are, however, plenty of DIY videos online that will show how to make quick work of this. My go-to method is to thinly slice off the top, make four vertical slits, pull apart the fruit into quarters and then gently pull out all the arils, discarding the membranes.

There is a method made famous by Nigella Lawson in which she turns halved pomegranates over a large bowl and taps them with a wooden spatula. This does lead to bruising of the arils and also splatters red juice on clothes and around the counter. Pomegranate juice is notorious for staining, due to which I prefer the neater first method.

1. Keeping shelled pomegranate in the fridge makes it easier to add to various dishes.
2. Add a handful of pomegranate to add sweetness and flavour to salads, chaats, and *raita*.
3. Pomegranate can also be added to fruit and vegetable juices along with beets and carrots.
4. Add a handful of pomegranate to smoothies.
5. Add pomegranate to a bowl of cereal or oatmeal.

POMELO / CITRUS MAXIMA

Nearly 50 compounds give the characteristic fragrance and flavour to a pomelo, the largest fruit from the citrus family, as is evident from its botanical name citrus maxima or citrus grandis. It also goes by the names of shaddock and pamplemousse.

There is a story that explains how this fruit came to be native to Devanahalli in the outskirts of Bengaluru. Mahatma Gandhi once came to Nandi Hills, the hill resort near Devanahalli and was offered a taste of this local fruit by a farmer named S.R. Channappa. He loved this fruit and advised Channappa to conserve this fruit variety. It was due to this that pomelo was distributed to farms all the way up to Chikmagalur, where it continues to grow today. Bihar, West Bengal, and other North-Eastern states also grow and consume pomelos.

Due to its presence in South-East Asian countries, you will find pomelo's delicate pink and fragrant presence in many salads, both vegetarian and combined with seafood. In Sri Lanka, pomelo sprinkled with sugar is eaten as dessert.

While using pomelo in salads, ensure it is handled with utmost lightness so as not to crush the fruit and release the juices. This turns the dish bitter if not consumed immediately.

Pranoy Thippaiah of Kerehaklu farms in Chikmagalur, grows pomelo trees as companion plants in his 275-acre coffee plantation. 'It is a huge fruit and it can feed three to four people. The large size is somewhat physically intimidating for a consumer to pick it up as a fruit for daily consumption. The popularity of pomelos is growing in India with features and recipes appearing in publications and magazines,' shares Thippaiah.

Nutrition in pomelo

Being a low-calorie fruit, pomelo can be enjoyed by weight watchers.

The fruit peel, as well as the pulp, is rich in antioxidants, such as vitamin C and lycopene. Vitamin C is a known antioxidant, which plays an important role in maintaining blood vessels, collagen, and cartilage. It is a vital nutrient for good skin as it has an impact on collagen production and in protecting skin from sun exposure. Lycopene is one of the most powerful heart-protective antioxidants.

Pomelos are a decent source of soluble fibre that dissolves in water in the gut and helps lower cholesterol and blood glucose levels.

Potassium in pomelo keeps blood vessels relaxed, thereby helping keep blood pressure under control, and is therefore useful for those with high blood pressure.

How to use

1. A regular-sized pomelo yields nearly six cups of edible fruit. Peel the fruit, discard the spongy pith, membranes, and seeds. Save the edible segments in airtight glass containers in the fridge. This can be used in various dishes for over two weeks.
2. Pomelo adds a delicate flavour, juiciness and sweetness to salads. Try the simple Assamese-style pomelo salad called *robab tenga* with sliced red chillies, salt and mustard oil.
3. Pomelos can also be added to stir-fries. Stir it in during the last few seconds of cooking. The addition of pomelo in a coconut milk-based spicy Thai curry offers a welcome relief when you bite into the mildly sweet fruit.
4. Pomelo can be added to smoothies and juices. Ginger and pomegranate are two of the ingredients that pair very well with pomelo.
5. Pomelo marmalade can be made in a similar method as ginger marmalade. The large seeds of pomelo are rich in pectin and can be used to naturally make the marmalade thick.

PUMPKIN

There are many varieties of pumpkins available in India – yellow, orange, and white being the most common ones.

Different varieties differ in their nutrient profiles. The darker orange and yellow varieties are rich in beta carotene. The white pumpkin, also called ash gourd, is very low in carbohydrates but high in water content. Different Indian cuisines and dishes have a preference for a certain variety, such as white pumpkin for *avial* and orange pumpkin for *kaddu ki sabzi*.

This section focuses on the orange and dark yellow coloured pumpkins.

If you end up buying a whole pumpkin, peel it and remove the seeds. Chop the pumpkin into cubes and either roast or boil the cubes in water to make a purée. The purée can be frozen in an ice cube tray and saved in resealable bags in the freezer. Pumpkin purée has uses in dozens of dishes, and it is an easy way to add the goodness of pumpkin into everyday cooking with almost zero effort.

Do not discard the skin or the seeds of the pumpkin. The skin can be sautéed along with spices and ground to a chutney along with coconut or what is called a *thogayal* in Tamil cooking. The seeds can be washed free of the membranes and dried out, some to be sowed in the kitchen garden and the rest to be oven roasted and had as a snack. The membranes and pith can go into the compost pile. This way the entire pumpkin from the skin to seed can be utilized with almost zero waste.

Nutrition in pumpkin

Pumpkin is low in calories due to its high water content. One cup of cooked pumpkin provides around 50 calories.

A cup of cooked pumpkin has over double the daily requirement of vitamin A. Vitamin A, along with lutein and zeaxanthin, helps with good vision. The bright orange colour of the pumpkin comes from beta carotene, which is the precursor to vitamin A. Beta carotene, along with vitamin E, prevents sun damage to the skin. Increased intake of alpha and beta carotene in the diet is linked to reduced incidence of stomach cancers[39] as well.

Pumpkin is rich in fibre too. A cup of cooked pumpkin provides around three grams of fibre.

Pumpkin is a good source of magnesium, which helps with nervous system regulation and muscle relaxation, and is a good food choice for those who work out a lot.

Pumpkin is also a good source of the amino acid tryptophan, which gets converted to the neurotransmitter serotonin that helps with unwinding and sleep.

Ways to cook pumpkin

Boiling method – Cut the pumpkin into cubes and boil for six to eight minutes in enough water until tender. This method works for soups, *sambars*, dals, etc.

Oven roasting – Toss pumpkin cubes in olive oil and salt, spread them in a single layer on a baking tray and bake at 180°C for 35–40 minutes until the cubes are tender. The time taken depends on the size of the cubes. This method works best for salads or to make puree for gnocchi or ravioli where no extra moisture is required.

Grating / spiralizing – Grated pumpkin can be microwaved for one minute or so until the pumpkin is slightly cooked and the raw edge is taken off. This works for salads and *raita*.

How to use

1. Used in bakes like muffins and tea cakes, it reduces the sugar and fat requirement in the recipe. It also results in moist cakes and muffins.
2. Added to a red pasta sauce, pumpkin purée takes the edge off the sourness from tomatoes while adding a creamy texture.
3. Pumpkin purée can be whisked into the egg-milk mixture for French toast.

4. Pumpkin purée enriches oatmeal porridge with a serving of vegetables and also adds flavour and creaminess.
5. It can be used to make pumpkin bread.
6. Thin down pumpkin purée with coconut milk and water. Blend with sautéed aromatics like garlic, onions and lots of ginger to make a pumpkin ginger soup.
7. Pumpkin purée can be used to make desserts like, mousse and cheesecake.
8. Mix pumpkin purée into blended chickpeas, olive oil, tahini, garlic and lemon juice to make pumpkin hummus.
9. Add a few cubes of frozen pumpkin purée into simmering dal. Use extra chillies or red chilli powder in the tempering to balance out the sweetness from the pumpkin.

RED GRAPES / VITIS VINIFERA

Archaeological evidence of winemaking has been found in China, Georgia, Iran, and Greece between 8,000 BCE and 4,500 BCE. Grapes were domesticated around 6,000–8,000 years ago. The earliest winery has been traced back to Armenia dating to roughly 4,000 BCE.

The process of winemaking from grapes coincides with the transition from a nomadic lifestyle to a settlement based lifestyle, where people could grow grapes, harvest them and allow time for them to ferment, which would at least take a week.

Grapes are classified as table grapes and wine grapes. Table grapes are larger sized seedless fruits with thinner skin. Wine grapes are smaller in size, seeded, sweeter and with a thicker skin. The aroma and flavour of the wine come from the skin.

Seedless grape varieties were obtained through selective propagation. They also came about due to a process of a natural mutation that stopped the immature seed in the grape from maturing and hardening. Seedless grapevines propagate through cuttings.

Quite a few people experience the misery of eating grapes and immediately coming down with a sore throat and cough. This is very likely an allergic reaction to one of the pesticides/ fungicides sprayed over the grapevines. Grapes are one of the produce that have the highest pesticide residue. Taking an over-the-counter antihistamine (anti-allergy medication) may help reduce the symptoms considerably. The other options are to buy organic grapes or follow a strict washing procedure for grapes using white vinegar and salt.

Grapeseed oil is gaining popularity in cooking as well as in the cosmetics industry. It is rich in vitamin E and polyunsaturated fatty acids.

Nutrition in red grapes

One cup of seedless grapes provides 62 calories and most of them come from sugars. Half a cup is the recommended serving size. Grapes are a good source of vitamins C and K. Vitamin C is vital for collagen production, serotonin production, and immunity. Vitamin K is important for blood clotting and bone health. Since Vitamin K is a fat soluble vitamin, it is advisable to combine red grapes with medium-fat yoghurt for a snack, for better absorption.

Grapes, although a high sugar fruit, have a low GI and can therefore be eaten by diabetics, with portion control. Some of the benefits of grapes are better blood sugar and insulin regulation and better insulin sensitivity[40], which could be a result of the many phytonutrients present in the fruit.

Red and black grapes are rich in the antioxidant resveratrol. They are known to reduce high cholesterol, high blood pressure, and reduce the risk of heart disease. Some studies also show a link between an increased intake of resveratrol rich foods to improve memory and cognitive function in older age groups.

Another antioxidant, called quercetin, is found in grapes, which is a powerful anti-inflammatory and antioxidant compound.

Grapes are rich in manganese, one of the trace minerals that play an important role in bone production, collagen production for skin integrity, antioxidants that protect skin from sun damage, and regulate blood sugar.

How to use

1. The best way to eat grapes is raw. Washed and chilled or frozen grapes make for a delicious snack, satisfying a sweet tooth as well.
2. Homemade focaccia stuffed with grapes and rosemary is full of flavour.
3. Add halved or whole grapes to a salad.
4. Grape jam tastes great on toast or parathas.
5. Grapes can be used to flavour *rasam*, by adding fresh grape juice just towards the end of simmering the dish.
6. Frozen grapes can be added to smoothies for natural sweetness.

What is the difference between red grapes and green grapes?

The colour of red or purple grapes is due to the presence of a polyphenol antioxidant called anthocyanin. In green grapes, a mutation prevents the compound anthocyanin from being produced. Due to this, the antioxidant value of green grapes is less than that of red grapes. The antioxidant value (ORAC) of red grapes is 1,837, while that of green grapes is 1,018. Raisins have an ORAC value of 3,400. One cup of raisins have eight times the calories of a cup of grapes, but realistically speaking it is not possible to eat a cup of raisins at a time. An ounce of raisins is a more realistic comparison to a cup of grapes and in this case, both are nutritionally similar.

SOYBEANS / GLYCINE MAX

Soybean is a legume and one of the important oilseeds with a global demand. According to a FICCI report[41] on the public-private partnership in the cultivation of soybeans in the state of Maharashtra, '[Soybeans] contributes 25 per cent to the global vegetable oil production, about two-thirds of the world's protein concentrate for livestock feeding and is a valuable ingredient in formulated feeds for poultry and fish.' It is a highly productive crop with good profit margins for the farmer. Being a legume, it also fixes nitrogen in the soil and improves soil quality for the next crop.

Mahatma Gandhi was an enthusiastic advocate of soybeans as a low-cost vegetarian protein. He was influenced by Narhar Bhave of Baroda, who went on to write a very popular book in 1936, *Soya Bean; Its Value in Dietetics, Cultivation and Uses*. The book has 375 pages of information on soybeans and 300 Indian, European, and East Asian recipes using soy foods.

As per a 2019 report published by the Soybean Processors Association of India, Rajasthan, Madhya Pradesh, and Maharashtra are the top three states that produce soybeans.

Textured vegetable protein (TVP) is one of the most popular ways soybean is consumed in India. It is one of the cheapest protein sources, and cooks in just a few minutes. Its neutral taste and spongy texture allow it to be used in a variety of savoury dishes, absorbing all the flavours in the dish. Because of its chewy texture, TVP chunks make for a good vegetarian or vegan substitute in meat-based dishes.

Soybeans are fermented to get soy sauce and tempeh. Fermented soybean paste is used as a condiment across east, south and South-East Asia. Two of the popular variants of the paste are *miso* in Japanese cuisine and *doenjang* in Korean cuisine. Versions of fermented soybean paste are also used in North-Eastern cooking in India, for example, *axone* from Nagaland (pronounced as 'akhuni').

Edamame is immature soybeans in pods. It is often found on the menu of Japanese restaurants, served either boiled or steamed in bamboo baskets topped with coarse salt.

Nutrition in soybeans

Soybeans are one of the few vegan/vegetarian sources of complete protein, having all nine essential amino acids. Around 100 grams of cooked soybeans provide over 16 grams of protein.

Among all the beans, this has the least carbohydrate and highest protein content. Fibre makes for a considerable portion of the carbohydrate content in the beans. Soybeans contain both soluble and insoluble fibre, which are good in preventing constipation, in blood sugar management and in reducing LDL cholesterol. It also acts as a prebiotic for the beneficial gut bacteria.

Soybeans are also a good source of calcium, iron, zinc, vitamin B, and omega 3 fatty acids.

A very important nutrient called isoflavones is present only in soybeans. These are plant-based oestrogens. In cultures where soy consumption is high, there is a lower incidence of hormone linked cancers of the breast, colon and prostate. Isoflavones also reduce the symptoms of menopause[42] such as hot flashes, mood swings and sweats; however, this is found mainly in people who have a gut bacteria that converts the isoflavones in soybeans to equol, which is responsible for the relief in menopause symptoms.

How to use

Soybeans are versatile because of their mild flavour. A point to note is that soybeans contain phytic acid, which is also called an anti-nutrient because it prevents the absorption of vital nutrients. The way to work around this is to follow the soak, sprout, ferment method, i.e., use either one or all of the methods while cooking with soybeans.

1. Soybeans can be ground to flour in your neighbourhood flour mill, or you can buy unprocessed soy flour to mix with wheat flour (atta) to make *rotis*. Replace 25 per cent of atta with soy flour to increase the protein and fibre content of *rotis* and parathas.
2. Baking flour can be fortified with 10 to 20 per cent of soy flour to make the baked good richer in protein.
3. A handful of soybeans can be added to *urad* dal that is soaked for *idli*/dosa batter.
4. *Adai* is a variety of thick dosa made from a mix of lentils, beans and rice, which are soaked then ground into a batter. Soybeans can be added to this mix of beans.
5. Soybeans can be roasted and ground along with other grains, beans and nuts to make a nutritious *kanji* (porridge) mix.

STRAWBERRIES / FRAGARIA ANANASSA

85 per cent of strawberries grown in India come from Mahabaleshwar, a hill station in western Maharashtra. It was to this summer capital of the Bombay Presidency. This is where the British brought strawberry saplings from Australia so that one of their favourite fruits could be grown locally. The strawberry farms are currently located in the Mahabaleshwar–Panchgani stretch. Many of these farms are open for berry picking in the season. Mapro was one such farm that set up a food processing unit in 1959 to make squashes and jam.

If summer belongs to mangoes, then winters in India surely belong to strawberries. Strawberries arrive with a splash in the peak winters and they are not very expensive, as compared to the other berries like blueberries, raspberries, and cranberries that are mostly imported. Technically speaking, strawberries are not berries as they belong to the rose family. Another interesting fact about this fruit is that it carries its seeds on the surface of the fruit and not inside it.

My childhood memories of strawberries include eating violently pink ice cream with an extremely artificial flavour that I loved nevertheless. Strawberry is one fruit which lends itself to every possible dessert. You may use them in shortcakes, teacakes, cupcakes, ice creams and so on. However, the healthy way to eat strawberries is as it is or in a smoothie, salad or a cold soup.

Nutrition in strawberries

Being low on calories and carbohydrates makes strawberries a good option for weight watchers.

It has a low GI (41) and minimal glycemic load (GL) of 1 (compare that with 16 in the case of figs). The GL of any food is the number that estimates how much that food will raise the blood glucose of a person after eating it. Research shows that eating strawberries makes the body use insulin more effectively, which means that less insulin is needed to manage the blood sugar after a meal. Adding strawberries to a high-carbohydrate meal seems to slow down the digestion of glucose from the meal, slowing down both insulin and blood glucose spikes, making it a valuable addition to a diabetic diet.

Strawberries are rich in vitamin C, with just five large berries supplying nearly 100 per cent of the daily value. Vitamin C is a powerful antioxidant, which also plays an important role in maintaining blood vessels, collagen, and cartilage. It is a vital nutrient for good skin as it has a positive impact on collagen production and protecting skin from sun exposure.

Folate found in strawberries is an extremely important vitamin to be consumed during pregnancy to prevent certain birth defects. It is also known for its cancer prevention properties.

Strawberries also provide potassium that keeps the blood vessels relaxed, thereby keeping blood pressure under control, and is useful for those with high blood pressure.

The antioxidants in strawberries reduce inflammation and oxidation of bad cholesterol, and also improve lipid profile and the functioning of blood vessels – all of which contribute towards a healthy heart.

All fruits and vegetables with a bright red and/or purple colour are rich in anthocyanins. Strawberries are a concentrated source of these compounds, unlike many fruits that only have the red pigments in the peels, most of which get discarded anyway. These phenolic antioxidants have immunity improving and cancer prevention properties[43].

How to use

1. A perfectly ripe strawberry is a delight to eat as it is.
2. These berries make a colourful addition to salads, also adding natural sweetness.
3. Strawberries can also be puréed to make a salad dressing along with lime juice and extra virgin olive oil.
4. Give the strawberries a quick wash, mop them dry, remove the green tops and lay them out on a baking tray in a single layer. Keep this in the freezer. Once frozen, store the strawberries in resealable plastic bags and keep them frozen for use in smoothies, sorbets, frozen yoghurt, etc. Frozen berries are not good for use in salads as they will lose their original texture on thawing.
5. Try making strawberry preserves along with chia seeds, to spread on toast or to serve with pancakes.

6. Strawberries dipped in melted dark chocolate is one of the healthiest desserts one can have.
7. Strawberries can be used in baking teacakes, muffins and cupcakes, but using it in recipes with a lot of added sugar negates all the health benefits that are gained from the fruit.

SUNFLOWER SEEDS / HELIANTHUS ANNUUS

Sunflowers are glorious blooms. One look at these bright yellow flowers and we can't help but feel cheery. Only when I grew sunflowers in my garden did I realize that the seeds form the head of the flower. The seed head of my sunflowers attracted all kinds of birds that love to feed on them. A single flower head may contain up to 2,000 seeds. Sunflowers are cultivated as a crop to extract oil from their seeds, which is a popular cooking medium in India due to its neutral flavour.

Sunflower seeds are available online as well as in organic stores, either with the shell on or removed. The ones with the shell, although higher in fibre and some B vitamins, are very coarse to eat and hard to digest. The ones with the shells removed are good for daily consumption as it is definitely easier to enjoy sunflower seeds this way. If buying roasted seeds, ensure that no extra oil and salt has been added to roast the seeds. Buying the raw shelled seeds and lightly toasting them at home is the best option.

Sunflower seeds, due to their high-fat content, turn rancid quickly, so buy them in small quantities or keep them in a sealed bag in the freezer.

Nutrition in sunflower seeds

A quarter cup of sunflower seeds has five-and-a-half grams protein and three grams of fibre. This makes it a good ingredient to add to flour-based breads as the fat, protein, and fibre slows down the absorption of glucose from such a seed-enriched bread.

A quarter cup of sunflower seeds provides 35 per cent of the daily requirement of vitamin E. Vitamin E is a powerful antioxidant, reducing oxidative damage in cell membranes, neurons and cholesterol molecules. It is interesting to note that vitamin E reduces the incidence of cardiovascular disease.

Being a fat-soluble antioxidant, it gets into cholesterol molecules, preventing the oxidation of cholesterol. Only when cholesterol is oxidized can it stick to walls of the blood vessels, depositing as plaques and leading to blockages, which in turn can lead to heart attacks or strokes. Making sure you get enough vitamin E in your diet is a good way to prevent the risk of atherosclerosis.

Vitamin E has been known to help in reducing perimenopausal symptoms like hot flashes and diabetes complications.

Sunflower seeds are rich in phytosterols that can be considered as plant-based cholesterol. When consumed, they are known to reduce blood cholesterol, benefit the immune system and reduce the incidence of certain cancers. Sesame seeds are the richest in phytosterols, but among the more snackable seeds and nuts, sunflower seeds and pistachios rank high.

Sunflower seeds are rich in vitamins B1 and B6, and selenium. Vitamin E and selenium work together to reduce inflammation[44] in the body.

The manganese in sunflower seeds plays an important role in bone production, collagen production for skin integrity, protecting the skin from sun damage, and blood sugar control.

It's commonly asked if sunflower seeds are rich in vitamin D, possibly due to its name. However, there is no vitamin D in sunflower seeds.

How to use

1. Snack healthy with sunflower seeds that have been roasted and salted or roasted with added spices.
2. Toasted sunflower seeds add a good crunch and a nutty flavour when used as an addition to salad. Add a sprinkle of sunflower seeds to the salad bowl just before eating so it retains its crunch.
3. Adding a spoonful of toasted sunflower seeds to a cup of soup adds texture.
4. Use sunflower seeds as a part of a toasted seed mix that can be used as a topping over a variety of dishes.
5. Adding sunflower seeds to baked goods like bread and muffins reduce the GI of the dish and make it more nutrient-rich.
6. Use it to make a savoury sunflower seed butter. This makes for a good change from peanut butter. Add savoury elements like herbs, smoked paprika, garlic powder and chillies to add lots of flavour.
7. Add sunflower seeds to the mix of lentils and seeds in *molagapodi*, the south Indian lentil powder that is eaten with all breakfast items. The regular *podi* can be given a boost with the addition of sunflower seeds, instead of or along with sesame seeds.
8. Use sunflower seeds instead of pine nuts along with basil, garlic and extra virgin olive oil to make pesto.
9. Peanuts or fried gram is often used as a thickener for chutneys. Toasted sunflower seeds can also be used for the same purpose.

10. A mix of fennel seeds, crushed coriander seeds, *ajwain* and sunflower seeds can be used as a mouth freshener or a healthy mix to munch on.
11. In Belarus, Russia, and Ukraine, roasted ground seeds are used to make a sweet fudge called *halva*. During the festive season, *laddoos* and Indian-style *halwas* can be made using sunflower seeds for a twist on the traditional nut-based sweets.

SWEET POTATO / IPOMOEA BATATAS

Although both potatoes and sweet potatoes are starchy root vegetables, botanically they are as different as day and night. Quite literally, sweet potatoes are from the morning glory family while potatoes are from the nightshade family. Both these root vegetables have their origins in South and Central America from where they migrated to places all around the world.

There is some debate over whether it is healthier to eat sweet potatoes rather than potatoes. Both tubers rank similarly in terms of calories, carbohydrate content and protein. Sweet potatoes are richer in vitamin A (especially the ones with darker-coloured flesh) and in fibre. Another important difference is the GI. A study found that the average GI of a boiled sweet potato, was 46 as compared to the baked sweet potato, which was 94, and a roasted sweet potato which was 82. The lower GI and the glycemic load (GL) of boiled sweet potatoes make it the healthiest way to cook this vegetable.

These values also depend on how the dish is prepared and what else is served with the ingredient. For example, mashed boiled sweet potato with white rice will have a much higher GI and GL than when it is mixed with protein-rich paneer and topped with seeds.

Sweet potato varieties vary in the colour of the skin and flesh. In India, the markets and supermarkets sell the variety with reddish skin and pale yellow flesh.

If a sweet potato is left in the kitchen for too long, the humid environment pushes the tuber to sprout which eventually sends out delicate stems and leaves. This can be kept in a pot of soil and grown as a houseplant to display leaves of pretty shape and colour. If buried in good quality soil, the sprouting sweet potato will take over the area and in around four months, new sweet potatoes can be dug out.

Nutrition in sweet potato

Sweet potatoes are rich in vitamin A. Mashed boiled sweet potatoes are a highly nutritious food to give to weaned babies and young children. Adding a bit of fat to this preparation by way of ghee or butter helps in better absorption of the fat-soluble vitamin.

Sweet potatoes are rich in vitamins C and B6. Vitamin C is a powerful antioxidant. It is also important for the production of collagen and the neurotransmitter serotonin. Our mood and sleep-wake cycles are influenced by this chemical. B6, or pyridoxine, is a water-soluble vitamin important for the production of red blood cells. It is one of the important vitamin B required for the production of neurotransmitters such as dopamine, serotonin, and GABA. It is also important for the metabolism of carbohydrates.

Sweet potatoes are a good source of manganese and copper. Manganese is one of the trace minerals that play an important role in bone production, collagen production for skin integrity, and antioxidants that protect skin from sun damage, and blood sugar control. Energy production, balancing cholesterol levels in the blood and collagen production (important for bone, skin and tissue integrity) are also some of the functions that depend on copper.

Anthocyanins in sweet potatoes are known for their anti-inflammatory benefits.

Resistant starch and fibre in sweet potato that reach the large intestine undigested, get fermented to produce short-chain fatty acids. These are said to prevent inflammation and offer protection from colon cancer.

The insoluble fibre in sweet potato helps prevent constipation. The soluble fibre helps in weight management, stabilizing sugar control and lowering cholesterol. It also acts as a prebiotic to feed the beneficial bacteria in the gut.

How to use

1. Boil and mash sweet potatoes to make baby food, or to prepare vegetable burgers.
2. Slice and sauté sweet potatoes to make a dry *sabzi*/curry. Finely dice the sweet potato and prepare a South Indian-style *poriyal* or *thoran* with a coconut garnish. The fat in the coconut helps absorb the fat-soluble vitamins.
3. Sweet potato slices can be oven-baked along with spices and a little oil for a healthy snack.
4. Make sweet potato fries in the air fryer. Spiralized noodles made from sweet potato can also be baked into a crunchy snack.
5. Roast chunks of sweet potato to add to a salad.
6. Thick slices of sweet potato can be used in *sambar*.

TAMARIND / TAMARINDUS INDICA

In most Indian cities and villages, you will find an ornamental canopy of a tamarind tree offering its shade to passers-by and capturing the mischief of young kids trying to get their hands on these tangy pods.

Tamarind is a tree with an average life of 100 years, but some even live on to be 200. It finds a place in the Food and Agricultural Organization of the United Nations' (UNFAO's) list of neglected and underutilized species (NUS). Tamarind was introduced to India in prehistoric times from its native, tropical Africa, and is now seen as indigenous to India. A mature tree produces 150–220 kilograms of fruit in a year.

The word tamarind is said to come from 'tamar hind' as it is called by the Persians and Arabs, meaning 'date of India'. Tamarind pods have a sweet pulp with added notes of sourness. Beyond culinary uses in the Indian subcontinent, tamarind is also an ingredient in some barbecue sauces and Worcestershire sauce. Tamarind-ade is a popular beverage in the South American countries of Guatemala, Mexico, and Puerto Rico.

Almost every part of the tamarind tree, such as the stem, bark, leaves, and fruit has uses in herbal medicine. In native medicine, tamarind pulp is applied as a remedy for inflamed skin. It is used in gargling for a sore throat and to combat sunstrokes, *datura* poisoning and alcoholic intoxication. Tamarind, in the form of a beverage, is used to treat gastrointestinal conditions like diarrhoea, constipation, and stomach ulcers. The bark and leaves are also used to promote wound healing.

Nutrition in tamarind

Tamarind is a good source of minerals like iron, selenium, potassium, magnesium, and copper. The 'carbohydrate-blocking' effect of tamarind, which may be helpful in keeping blood sugars under check in diabetics, is still a subject of research. Magnesium is also linked to a lower risk of Type II diabetes. Magnesium is also a key factor in bone health, heart health, and preventing and relieving migraine headaches.

Tamarind is a good source of thiamine or vitamin B1, which plays an important role in glucose metabolism and in using carbohydrates in the diet for energy. Thiamine is also vital for nerve, muscle and heart functioning.

The phenolic compounds (flavonoids) in tamarind have shown to have antioxidant and anti-inflammatory[45] properties. These can protect against diseases such as heart disease, cancer and diabetes.

The tamarind seed extract may help lower blood sugar and have an anti-arthritic effect[46] and the pulp extract may help reduce weight and reverse fatty liver.

How to use

1. Readymade tamarind paste for quick use in Indian curries and sauces is an easy way to use tamarind in cooking. Do note that it may contain salt and other preservatives, and may not provide an authentic tamarind flavour to traditional dishes.
2. The best way to use tamarind is to buy the cleaned pods which have been pressed into blocks. There may be a stray seed or two in these pods. Soak the required quantity of tamarind in hot water for 15 minutes and extract the pulp by squeezing the pods. The soaking time depends on how fresh or dried the pods are. This extract can be used to sour curries and dals, and to make *sambar* and *rasam*.
3. Tamarind can be boiled down to a thicker consistency along with date puree and spices to make a sweet chutney called *saunth* that is ubiquitous in north Indian chaats.
4. *Imli ki goli,* a tamarind-based candy, is a popular after-meal digestive in India.
5. Use tamarind extract or pulp as the acidic ingredient in salad dressings and condiments such as satay sauce.

TOMATO / SOLANUM LYCOPERSICUM

Tomatoes are botanically a fruit, more specifically a berry, but recognized as a vegetable for culinary purposes. Given how much we use tomatoes in Indian cuisine, it is surprising to know that tomatoes were introduced to India rather recently. According to the book, *A Historical Dictionary of Indian Food*, by K.T. Achaya, 'unlike several other plants from the New world, the tomato did not come directly to India, but by the way of England at a late but uncertain date perhaps around 1850'. Thus, we have been using tomatoes in the Indian cuisine only for the last 170 years. That explains why we still have a lot of traditional recipes that do not use tomatoes. The Indian kitchen also has a number of other souring agents to add flavour and freshness to dishes, such as tamarind, ***kokum***, amchoor, yoghurt, etc. Even though present-day Italian cuisine is rather unimaginable without tomatoes, they were introduced to Italy as late as mid-16th century.

Cooked down tomatoes, along with ginger, garlic, and onions, form the backbone of the 'bhuna' gravy. The umami flavour of tomatoes is harnessed in pickles and chutneys. Tomato soup (with ghee-fried croutons) was probably the most commonly ordered dish in restaurants in the pre-2000 era.

It is the one vegetable that features in a very popular cocktail – the Bloody Mary–which has vodka along with tomato juice, hot sauce, horseradish, and celery. Tomato ketchup, which is probably the world's most popular condiment, has its origins in China – kê-tsiap, a fermented fish sauce. The first published recipe for tomato ketchup appeared in 1812 and it went through a lot of changes until it started to be commercially manufactured in America by Heinz in 1876.

Tomatoes have a large number of species that vary in flavour profile, the thickness of the skin, the quantity of pulp and seeds, etc. Each type of tomato is cultivated for a specific purpose. It is often the first vegetable (or fruit) grown by a kitchen gardener.

Nutrition in tomatoes

The most important reason to eat tomatoes is the presence of lycopene, a phytochemical that gives tomatoes its red colour. It is a powerful heart-healthy antioxidant. While most fruits and vegetables have a better nutritional profile when eaten raw, an exception to the rule is lycopene in tomatoes. Cooked tomatoes have higher lycopene than uncooked tomatoes. Lycopene also reduces the risk of cancer. Studies have shown that cooking tomatoes at 88°C for 30 minutes increases its trans lycopene content by 164 per cent[47]. Heating does reduce the vitamin C content of the tomatoes though.

Tomato is a good source of insoluble fibre. This makes it a very good prebiotic for the beneficial gut bacteria.

Tomatoes are a good source of vitamins A and C, and folic acid, all of which are potent antioxidants. Vitamin C-rich tomatoes are very good for skin health due to its role in collagen production and in the protection of the skin from UV rays.

The combination of lycopene, lutein, and beta carotene makes tomatoes very good for eye health.

How to use

1. Tomatoes can be used as a curry base to prepare many north Indian-style gravy dishes.
2. Use it to make chutneys paired with onions and garlic to go with *idlis* and *dosas*.
3. Tomato-based pasta sauce can be prepared in bulk when tomatoes are in season and full of flavour.
4. Finely chopped tomatoes with onion, chillies, and olive oil yield a flavoursome salsa.
5. Fresh tomatoes can be used in bruschetta, salads, and sandwiches.
6. The Indian salad (i.e., *kachumber*) can be made with fresh tomatoes, onions, and cucumber with a sprinkle of red chilli powder, salt, and lime juice.

TURMERIC / CURCUMA LONGA

'A vegetable which has all the properties of the true saffron, as well as the colour, and yet it is not really saffron'— this was how Marco Polo described turmeric while writing about his travels in China in the 13th century.

Come fresh turmeric season, my maternal grandmother used to bury a part of the root in a recycled pot, and like magic, the fragrant leaves of the turmeric plant would come out in a few weeks. New roots would form in the soil all set to be pulled out in three to four months, just in time for Pongal, the harvest festival celebrated by Tamil folk. The entire plant, root, leaves and all, would be tied around the neck of a brass cooking pot in which the dish *pongal* was prepared for the auspicious day.

India is the largest producer of turmeric in the world – 80 per cent of the world's turmeric is grown in India, out of which 92 per cent is consumed locally and 8 per cent is exported for staff. To quote Camellia Panjabi from *The Great Curries of India*, 'The largest turmeric production is around the town of Erode in Tamil Nadu, in Andhra and Maharashtra. That which gives the brightest hue is from around Alleppey in Kerala. The biggest turmeric market in the world is in Sangli where the turmeric is stored in large pits in the ground.'

Lakadong is a village in the West Jaintia Hills of Meghalaya and the turmeric grown here is said to have the highest concentration of curcumin (between six to seven and a half per cent), the active ingredient responsible for the health benefits of turmeric. The state has launched a program called 'Mission Lakadong' that aims to produce 50,000 metric tonnes of Lakadong turmeric between the years 2018 and 2023.

Fresh turmeric is available between December and February. Since turmeric powder is one of the most commonly adulterated spices, it is best to buy the dried root when it is in season and grind it to a powder either in a high-powered mixer at home or in a flour mill that also grinds spices. This powder can be stocked up for the whole year in the refrigerator or freezer.

In Mangalorean, Goan, Maharashtrian, and Konkani cuisine, turmeric leaves are used to wrap and steam foods, which impart a unique flavour to the dish. This method is used mostly in places that grow turmeric and therefore have access to leaves.

Nutrition in turmeric

The polyphenol compound curcumin is the active ingredient in turmeric. Absorption of curcumin is increased 2,000-fold in the presence of piperine, the active ingredient in black pepper. Health supplements usually have a combination of both. Curcumin is a fat-soluble compound which explains why turmeric is usually stirred into warm oil in the *tadka* (it burns when added to oil that is too hot).

Curcumin is a potent antioxidant that not only fights free radical damage but also has anti-inflammatory properties. These two properties combined have health benefits that impact the heart, kidneys, eyes, and bones. They combat osteoarthritis and general inflammatory conditions[48, 49]. They also reduce pain and improve symptoms of metabolic syndrome.

Turmeric is also said to reduce angiogenesis[50], i.e., the formation of new blood vessels, thereby reducing cancer risk.

Turmeric has many other pharmacologically active substances. However, studies to prove a relationship between tumeric and Alzheimer's disease and several cancers are ongoing.

How to use

1. The fresh root can be used in smoothies, teas, turmeric milk, curries, salads, pickles and curry pastes.

2. Try a simple pickle with fresh turmeric root. Peel and chop the root. Transfer to a glass jar. Cover it with lemon juice, salt and chopped green chillies. This quick pickle will be ready in two to three days.
3. Turmeric powder is used in many savoury Indian dishes for its colour and flavour, such as in dal, curries, *khichdi*, etc.
4. Turmeric powder can be used in smoothies and in turmeric milk.
5. When using turmeric powder in salad dressings, use some honey to neutralize its bitter notes.

WATERMELON / CITRULLUS LANATUS

Watermelon sits right up there at the intersection of healthy and delicious. A sweet juicy indulgence on hot days, eaten on its own or for use in juices and salads, it is easy to love and consume this fruit by the kilo. Eating it as it is poses no problems as the seeds can be removed and kept aside, but adding watermelon to salads and juices with the seeds intact makes for an unpleasant eating experience. You will find many videos on the internet on how to quickly deseed a watermelon. Find one that works for you. I can tell from experience that a big watermelon can be completely deseeded and cubed in just two minutes.

Watermelons are warm climate crops and can be grown around the year in Tamil Nadu, Andhra Pradesh, Odisha, Karnataka, etc., where there is no risk of frost. Its harvest coincides with the hot summer months in India, making it most useful when one wants to stay hydrated.

Nutrition in watermelon

Watermelon is a good source of the powerful antioxidant lycopene. A 100 grams (roughly two-thirds of a cup) provides 4–5 milligrams of lycopene. Comparatively, red tomatoes provide 3–4 milligrams per 100 grams. It has been found that the lycopene from watermelons is better absorbed than that from tomatoes.

Watermelon is also rich in vitamin C, which contributes to reducing inflammation, better skin health, and better immunity.

According to researchers at Sorbonne University, France, watermelons contain the amino acid L citrullinne,[52] which helps burn 13 per cent more body fat and builds nine per cent more muscle size as compared to amino acids. It stimulates regenerative proteins that build muscle and repair the mitochondria, thereby producing more energy and burning more fat. Arginine and citrulline are amino acids that improve the production of nitric oxide, which keeps the blood vessels relaxed. This, in turn, keeps the blood pressure under control and prevents heart disease.

Watermelons are also a good source of copper, biotin, potassium, vitamins A (in the form of carotenoids), B1, B6, and magnesium.

How to use

1. Choose a fruit that is heavy for its size. A yellow or pale spot on one side indicates its contact with the soil or ground and that it will most likely have ripe red flesh. The ones with the red flesh have the most antioxidants.
2. Cubed watermelon can be eaten as it is or in combination with other fruits.
3. Add a mix of vegetables and leafy greens to cubed watermelon to make juice or a smoothie.
4. Use watermelon in combination with cucumber and tomatoes in a gazpacho topped with extra virgin olive oil and black pepper.
5. Watermelon puree can be added to a lentil soup just before taking it off the heat, which makes a tasty *rasam*.

6. Cubed watermelon makes for a sweet and juicy addition to salads in combination with mint and feta cheese.
7. Watermelon rind can be used in Indian curries and *koottu* (in combination with dal). Choose an organic variety of watermelon for this purpose.
8. Watermelon seeds can be toasted in combination with other seeds and used as a topping for salads, soups and smoothies.

WHEATGRASS

When this superfood became a household name in the 1990s, I remember my father preparing seven pots of soil for sowing wheat and hanging them using fabricated rods to the grill of our Mumbai apartment. The grass was trimmed from one pot every day of the week. By the next week, the first pot was again ready for harvest. This home production of wheatgrass stopped when wheatgrass juice started getting delivered to our doorstep at at 5 AM each morning by enterprising businesses, the way it happens only in Mumbai.

What exactly is wheatgrass? Wheat grains are soaked, sprouted, and sowed to give off shoots which look like grass. These are microgreens harvested for their high levels of chlorophyll, to be consumed as a raw juice.

A common doubt regarding wheatgrass is whether the juice and powder are gluten-free and if they are suitable for those following a gluten-free diet. The answer is yes. The grass itself is gluten-free as long as it is carefully snipped only to include the blades of grass and not the seed (wheat grain) itself. When buying the powder, take note of the label to be sure that it is certified as gluten-free.

Nutrition in wheatgrass

Wheatgrass is rich in iron, calcium, enzymes, chlorophyll and almost all vitamins. Chlorophyll increases the red blood cell count and is a very good natural supplement for those who have anaemia.

Wheatgrass is said to lower blood sugar levels as it mimics insulin and lowers the GI of foods that it is consumed with.

Mouth cancer cells treated with a wheatgrass preparation in a lab showed a slowdown in the growth of cancer cells[53], indicating that this superfood may have a favourable impact on preventing and treating cancer. Studies have shown that wheatgrass helps improve the response to chemotherapy[54] as well.

As it is potent with several micronutrients, a small dose of 30 ml of wheatgrass juice is recommended. If it causes any side effects like nausea, it can be diluted with a glass of water. While it is recommended to drink this on an empty stomach for better absorption of nutrients, if it causes any side effects like nausea or acidity, then having wheatgrass with breakfast is a good idea. Fats in breakfast will also help better absorb the fat-soluble vitamins in the drink.

Wheatgrass is definitely a very strong and acquired taste, and is not a drink that can be sipped and savoured. Given that the dosage is small, it is easier to just gulp it down.

How to use

1. Wheatgrass can be blended in the mixer with a little water to make wheatgrass juice. There are a few ingredients–honey, ginger juice, lemon juice, orange juice and amla juice—that work well in combination with wheatgrass juice, by improving absorption of its nutrients and by masking the somewhat metallic flavour. Use one or two of these ingredients in combination with 30 ml of the wheatgrass juice.
2. Packets of snipped wheatgrass are available in many supermarkets and health food stores. It is also available in the form of a capsule.

3. Fresh wheatgrass has a very short shelf life which is why wheatgrass powder is a good alternative for regular consumption. Mixed into water or had as a smoothie, it has a similar effect as consuming fresh wheatgrass juice. (For more information on superfood powders, refer to the namesake section on page 168)

5

Specific Superfoods

A study done by the National Institute of Nutrition in Hydrebad assessed the blood levels of vitamins (A, B1, B2, B6, B12, folic acid, and D) and homocysteine in 270 healthy adults between the age of 30 and 70. The study revealed a vitamin B2 (riboflavin) deficiency in 50 per cent of the people, followed by a vitamin B6 deficiency in 46 per cent. These deficiencies are mainly due to poor intake of nutrient-rich foods. Vitamin D deficiency could also be seen due to lesser exposure to sunlight in urban areas. Low levels of vitamin B12 and folic acid lead to increased levels of homocysteine, which is responsible for various conditions like bone thinning, the build-up of plaque in walls of arteries, clots in blood vessels, coronary artery disease, and stroke. This study concluded a high prevalence of multiple subclinical vitamin deficiencies. The dietary shortfall of these vitamins is a possible risk factor for many chronic diseases among relatively healthy adults.

Vitamins and minerals are required in very small quantities in our daily diet; therefore, they are categorized as micronutrients. Vitamins are organic substances manufactured by living things like plants and animals. They are delicate compounds that can be easily destroyed or deactivated during cooking with heat, or exposure to air for longer periods. Minerals, on the other hand, are simple inorganic substances present in soil and water. They are not destroyed by heat, light, or chemical reactions. Plants absorb minerals from the soil they grow in and we, in turn, get the minerals from these plants (vegetables and fruits) we eat. All vitamins are essential for a healthy body while only some of the minerals are considered essential. Together, they work to carry out innumerable functions in the body, some of them being preventing birth defects, keeping the immune system in good shape, wound healing, bone health, sugar metabolism, repairing and preventing cellular damage.

Vitamins can further be divided into water-soluble and fat-soluble. Water-soluble vitamins are directly absorbed from food as they get broken down during digestion. These vitamins metabolize quickly, and any excess is flushed out by the kidneys through urine, which is why regular consumption in the diet is essential. While water-soluble vitamins (B and C) are vital for many specific tasks in the body, the most important ones being producing energy, releasing energy, building proteins and cells, and building collagen. Vitamin C is very important in collagen synthesis which aids wound healing, forms the wall of blood vessels and a framework for teeth and bones.

Fat-soluble vitamins, as the name suggests, do not dissolve in water, but in fats. These are best absorbed when eaten along with fats in a meal. They are found in fatty foods like oily fish, dairy products, egg yolks, and organ meat like liver. Any excess fat-soluble vitamins do not get flushed out in the urine but are stored in the liver and fat tissues. As and when these vitamins are required, they are released from storage into the bloodstream, which is why a daily intake of these vitamins is not needed. Some of the important roles of fat-soluble vitamins are bone-building, eyesight, and antioxidant properties. As these vitamins are stored by the body, consuming them as supplements over a long period of time can lead to build-up and toxicity.

Like vitamins, minerals can also be further divided into two distinct groups – major and minor minerals. As the name suggests, larger quantities of major minerals are required in the diet while only small quantities of trace minerals are needed.

Table 5.1 Vitamins and Minerals

Water-soluble vitamins	Fat-soluble vitamins	Major minerals	Trace minerals
Vitamin B1 (Thiamine)	Vitamin A	Calcium	Chromium
Vitamin B2 (Riboflavin)	Vitamin D	Chloride	Copper
Vitamin B3 (Niacin)	Vitamin E	Magnesium	Fluoride
Vitamin B5 (Pantothenic Acid)	Vitamin K	Phosphorus	Iodine
Vitamin B6 (Pyridoxine)		Sodium	Iron
Vitamin B7 (Biotin)		Sulphur	Manganese
Vitamin B9 (folic acid)			Molybdenum
Vitamin B12 (cobalamin)			Selenium
Vitamin C			Zinc

These micronutrients do not function in isolation; there is a lot of interplay between them. To gives some examples, vitamin C helps in the absorption of iron vitamin D helps the body to absorb calcium from food sources rather than leaching it from the bones. Copper absorption is decreased in the presence of calcium, iron, and vitamin C.

A few essential vitamins and minerals are listed in Table 5.2 along with their major food sources.

Table 5.2: Essential Vitamins and Minerals with their Major Food Sources

Nutrient	Importance	Sources
Vitamin B2	• Important for the breakdown of carbohydrates, proteins and fats • Absorption of other nutrients • Maintaining tissue integrity	• Whole-grain bread • Yoghurt • Peas • Spinach • Sweet potato • Broccoli • Wheat bran • Nuts • Avocados • Mushrooms
Vitamin B6	• Important role in the central nervous system for the production of neurotransmitters and hormones like serotonin and norepinephrine • Important for protein metabolism and glucose metabolism • Production of haemoglobin in red blood cells	• Boiled potatoes • Banana • Garlic • Paneer • Chickpeas • Watermelon • Pistachio • Meat-based sources like chicken breast, salmon, turkey

Nutrient	Importance	Sources
Vitamin B9 (folic acid)	• Required for manufacturing white blood cells and red blood cells in the bone marrow • Important role in DNA and RNA formation and in converting carbohydrates into energy • Vital for a healthy pregnancy (in reducing congenital birth defects) and during adolescence and infancy • It is also believed that folic acid gradually relieves or prevents depression	• Lentils • Ladyfinger • Broccoli • Spinach • Legumes like black-eyed peas, kidney beans, peas • Green leafy vegetables • Beetroot • Orange • Broccoli • Avocado
Vitamin B12	• Required for proper red blood cell formation, neurological function and DNA synthesis • *Note:* Deficiency can lead to cardiovascular disease, dementia and low energy levels	• Milk • Yoghurt • Cheese • Eggs • Seafood and meat-based sources like clams and beef liver • Vitamin B12 fortified foods, nutritional yeast or daily/weekly supplement are some vegan options

Nutrient	Importance	Sources
Vitamin A	• Important for vision and immunity • Cellular and body growth • Healthy hair • Important role in reproductive functions	• Vitamin A is present only in animal sources like dairy, liver and fish oil • Plant sources like orange, yellow and red coloured fruits and vegetables, DGLVs, sweet potatoes, broccoli, etc., contain beta carotene from which vitamin A is derived
Vitamin D	• Important for healthy bones and teeth, immune system, brain and nervous system • Improves insulin sensitivity, better diabetes management • Important for lung function and cardiovascular health • A powerful antioxidant	• Exposure to sunlight • Shitake mushrooms and fortified foods are some of the vegan options • Fortified milk and eggs • Cod liver oil supplements, salmon and canned tuna are some of the fish-based sources

Nutrient	Importance	Sources
Iron	• An essential component of haemoglobin, transporting oxygen from lungs to tissues • Required for a healthy pregnancy, good energy levels and athletic performance	• Spinach • Legumes • Pumpkin seeds • Quinoa • Broccoli • Tofu • Dark chocolate • Liver and other organ meats, red meat and turkey are the meat-based sources • *Note:* although there are many dietary sources for iron, there are also a number of factors that prevent absorption such as intake of antacids, polyphenols in cereal, pulses and spinach, tannins in tea and wine, phytates in beans and whole grains
Calcium	• An essential mineral for strong bones and teeth, for muscle contractions and for blood clotting	• Milk • Cheese • Yoghurt • Tofu • Beans • Figs • Broccoli • Nuts and seeds • *Note:* Calcium needs the presence of vitamin D for its absorption. Some DGLVs have a higher concentration of oxalic acid that prevents the absorption of calcium

Specific superfoods

While eating a variety of superfoods as a part of your daily diet is a great way to maintain good health, superfoods that are rich in certain nutrients help with specific conditions as described below.

Weight loss

The simplest way to look at weight loss is 'calories in and calories out'. Of course, it is way more complicated than that. In general, some food rules do work when it comes to weight loss.

Foods to focus on

- Fill up on low-calorie vegetable dishes made from cauliflower, broccoli, bell peppers, mushrooms, bean sprouts, cabbage, gourds and squashes, eggplant, green leafy vegetables.
- Eat high-fibre foods such as a variety of beans and lentils, fibre-rich fruits, and green leafy vegetables that keep blood sugar levels stable and provide better satiety.
- Eat foods with resistant starch[1]—green bananas, legumes, rice and potatoes—after cooking and refrigerating overnight as it helps reduce appetite and makes one feel fuller for longer.
- Avoid food and drinks with added sugar as well as highly refined or processed foods that not only add empty calories but also play havoc with insulin levels.

Diabetes

If there is one condition that is intrinsically linked to the food we eat, it is Type II diabetes. In most cases, poor lifestyle and bad food habits cause Type II diabetes. A high-fibre diet, rich in plant protein, moderate in whole grains and devoid of processed flours and sugars is a good broad guideline to follow. Choosing foods with a low GI ensures that the blood sugar does not have sharp spikes after a meal.

Foods to focus on

- Beans are high in fibre, protein, magnesium, and potassium, with a lower GI.
- Nuts and seeds contain healthy fats that are rich in omega-3 fatty acids, zinc, and vitamins.
- Pomelo, oranges, limes and other citrus fruits are low in GI and rich in vitamin C, folic acid, and fibre. Choose whole fruits and not fruit juices.
- Tomatoes are rich in vitamin C, vitamin E, potassium and lycopene (in cooked tomatoes) that help reduce blood pressure which, in turn, reduces the risk of cardiovascular disease associated with diabetes.
- *Amla* has antioxidant and anti-inflammatory properties, both very important for preventing diabetes-related complications.
- Whole grains such as, unpolished or minimally polished rice, barley, quinoa, amaranth, and millets are rich in vitamin B, folic acid, iron, chromium, and magnesium, along with beneficial soluble and insoluble fibre.
- All low-carb vegetables, including green leafy vegetables, supply vital micronutrients while providing fibre and satiety.
- Starchy vegetables and high sugar fruits should be eaten in moderation or along with a balanced meal.
- Sugar, refined flour and processed foods to be consumed minimally.

Heart disease

While eating a healthy diet full of whole and natural foods is good for heart health, there are certain foods that are beneficial in preventing or helping with specific symptoms of heart disease such as increased levels of bad cholesterol, atherosclerosis, high blood pressure, and inflammation.

Foods to focus on

- Whole grains (and pseudo-grains), such as unpolished rice, millets, quinoa, amaranth, barley, buckwheat, steel-cut oats, etc., contain soluble fibre and prevent the absorption of cholesterol in the body.
- Beans and lentils are plant proteins that provide soluble fibre that lowers LDL (low-density lipoprotein) cholesterol.
- Nuts and seeds such as walnuts, almonds, chia seeds and flax seeds provide vitamin E (a powerful antioxidant), omega-3 fatty acids (reduces triglyceride cholesterol levels), minerals, and soluble fibre.
- Strawberries and other bright coloured fruits and vegetables, as well as dark chocolate, are rich in flavonoids that reduce blood pressure and improve circulation.
- Vitamin C-rich fruits like citrus, *amla*, guava, etc., lower the risk of heart disease and stroke. Potassium in the fruits helps balance blood pressure.
- Vitamin C and folic acid-rich vegetables such as cabbage, cauliflower, broccoli, and bok choy reduce the risk of heart disease.

Cancer prevention

A combination of anti-angiogenic foods and free-radical-fighting, antioxidant-rich foods work well for cancer prevention. Tumours need growth of new blood vessels to supply both nutrients and oxygen. Anti-angiogenesis means inhibiting the growth of new blood vessels which, in turns, cuts off the supplies that a tumour needs for its growth.

Dr. William Li in his TED Talk, 'Can we eat to starve cancer', explains how the human body forms microscopic cancer cells all the time, but these can grow into harmful cancer only with blood supply, i.e., angiogenesis. Thus, eating a number of anti-angiogenic foods in the diet is one of the best ways to prevent cancers.

Foods to focus on
Here are some of the superfoods that have an anti-angiogenic effect, along with a powerful antioxidant effect.

- Fruits: Strawberries, blueberries, orange, grapefruit, lemon, apple, pineapple, cherries, red grapes
- Vegetables: Tomato, bok choy, kale, pumpkin
- Green tea, red wine, olive oil, grape seed oil, dark chocolate
- Garlic, parsley, lavender, turmeric, nutmeg, soybean

According to the Angiogenesis Foundation, including as many of these foods in your diet on a regular basis is bound to have a beneficial effect.

Digestive health
Our gut is host to nearly 40 trillion bacteria. According to a 2019 report published in *Psychology Today*, gut bacteria can influence our mood, thoughts, and brain[2]. The good bacteria in the gut help with digestion, the absorption of vital nutrients, and the synthesis of vitamins. They also contribute towards immunity.

Gut health is entirely dictated by what we eat and drink. It is, therefore, easy to improve the gut microbiome by eating certain foods and avoiding certain other foods.

Foods to focus on
Important categories of foods for digestive health are high-fibre foods and fermented foods. Probiotics and prebiotics

play a very important role in gut health. Probiotics are the beneficial gut bacteria and prebiotics provide food for the friendly gut bacteria.

- Prebiotics: Fibre-rich beans, fruits, vegetables
- Probiotics: Overnight oats, overnight-rice mixed with yoghurt (*pakhala bhaat / pazhaidhu saadham*), kombucha, yoghurt, kimchi
- Focus on eating more insoluble fibre-rich foods, like whole grains, beans, fruits and vegetables that increase the bulk of the stools and prevent constipation.

Sugar and artificial sweeteners disturb the balance of the gut microbes, leading to poor gut health. Antibiotic therapies can also deplete the colonies of good bacteria.

Skin and hair

Healthy skin and hair depend more on what we eat than what we apply on them externally. Iron deficiency, vitamin D deficiency, zinc deficiency, low levels of thyroid hormone, other hormonal changes, change in metabolism, low-calorie diets with a decreased protein intake, and poor sleep habits can all cause hair loss. Poor hydration can make the skin look dry and dull. While a lot of other factors affect our hair and skin such as genetics, hormones, age and weather, one factor that can be controlled by us is our diet.

Foods to focus on

- Food like broccoli, spinach, *amla*, guava, citrus fruits, tomatoes, bell peppers that are a good source of vitamin C boost the growth of collagen in the skin.
- Nuts and seeds are rich in vitamin E, a powerful antioxidant that helps repair skin and offers protection from the sun's harmful UV rays.

- Pomegranate contains ellagic acid, a powerful polyphenol that helps prevent collagen breakdown and the inflammation caused by UVB rays.
- Orange, yellow and red-coloured fruits and vegetables are rich in beta carotene, which gets converted to vitamin A that provides skin elasticity and cell regeneration, both of which give a youthful-looking skin.
- Avocado is rich in vitamin A and healthy fats. It can also be used as a face mask. Rub the inside of the peels with leftover avocado flesh on the skin and neck. Allow it to dry for 15 minutes and wash off with water for a soft and moisturized skin.
- Lycopene in cooked tomatoes and watermelons has an antiaging effect on the skin, reducing inflammation, boosting cell renewal, and reducing damage by UV rays.
- Hydration is extremely important for skin health.
- Biotin-rich foods such as eggs, almonds, cheese, cauliflower, mushroom, and sweet potato are good for healthy hair.
- Protein-rich foods such as beans, lentils, tofu, dairy, quinoa, eggs, fish, etc., are also important for healthy hair growth.

Immunity

Immunity can be defined as a complex biological system endowed with the capacity to recognize and tolerate whatever belongs to the self, and to recognize and reject what is foreign (non-self). In simpler terms, immunity is the body's ability to prevent or fight infections. The components of the immune system are organs (spleen, thymus, bone marrow), lymphatic system, white blood cells, antibodies, and the complement system. Given that immunity works in a complex manner, there is no single magic solution to boost immunity. A combination of an overall healthy diet rich in fruits and vegetables, regular physical activity, adequate sleep, proper handwashing, and not smoking has a positive impact on immunity.

Foods to focus on

Following are certain foods which are believed to boost the immune system either by providing protein for the building blocks of cells and antibodies or via antioxidants that fight free radicals and food rich in specific micronutrients:

- Protein-rich foods such as eggs, lean meat, nuts/seeds, dairy, legumes, and tofu.
- Spices such as turmeric and black pepper for their antioxidant active ingredients.
- Garlic and onions, and other compounds that are rich in sulphur as they have antibiotic-like properties. It is best to consume them raw.
- Vitamin C-rich foods like amla, citrus, and guava.
- Omega-3 rich foods such as hemp seeds, chia seeds, flax seeds, salmon.
- Zinc-rich foods such as seeds and whole grains.
- Prebiotic foods like onion, banana, apple, mushrooms, oats, and barley that provide fuel for the healthy bacteria in the gut along with gut-friendly probiotics like yoghurt.

Superfoods for children

The first step in tackling children's nutritional needs is educating them. As children spend more of their time either at school or playing, which are outside the boundaries of our watch and care, they need to be empowered to make good food choices for themselves. Children should be taught what comprises real nutrition, why certain foods should be occasional treats and not a part of our daily shopping or consumption. Teach them about whole grains, proteins, healthy fats and micronutrients.

What works better than explaining to them is setting an example for them. Kids learn better by watching what their parents (or role models) do. By sticking to good food habits, like eating plenty of whole foods, making an effort to buy unprocessed foods, cooking as a family, sitting down together at a table for meals, sharing meals with friends and community, working together on a little kitchen garden or a windowsill garden are all lasting ways to help them build a healthy relationship with food.

Foods to focus on

- **Protein-rich foods** such as legumes, lentils, milk, yoghurt, cheese, paneer, tofu and eggs are important for growing muscles and bones. These foods also provide calcium that is vital for bone growth. Depending on dietary habits, add other lean meats as a supplementary protein source.
  Serving ideas:
  - ◊ Curries and salads made using legumes.
  - ◊ Eggs in any form for breakfast.
  - ◊ Tofu in stir-fries along with seasonal vegetables.
  - ◊ Plain homemade yoghurt with a spoonful of any pure fruit preserve or chopped fruits, or combined with rice to make curd rice, or served with muesli or cereal.
  - ◊ Cheese in salads, sandwiches, parathas.
  - ◊ Paneer in curries, parathas, sandwich stuffing.

- Since children tend to catch colds and flu regularly from close contact with each other at school and play, include vitamin C-rich foods such as citrus fruits, guava, cauliflower, bell peppers, spinach, tomatoes, and watermelon in their diet to keep the immunity in good shape.
  Serving ideas:
  - ◊ Make it a habit to give children one or two seasonal fruits every day, including a vitamin C-rich fruit.

◊ Watermelon can be mixed along with other fruits or vegetables to make a soup or cubes of watermelon can be given as an after-play refreshing snack.
◊ Make a large batch of pasta sauce when tomatoes are in season. Use it in sandwiches and pasta, or toss them in beans, rice or over a pizza. Kids love the taste of tomato-based pasta sauce and this is an excellent way to give them a dose of vitamin C and lycopene, which are powerful antioxidants.
◊ Add bell peppers to pasta, and in sandwiches and salads.
◊ Add spinach or other green leafy vegetables to paneer or any curry or dal.

- **Immunity boosting foods** such as *amla* and turmeric.
  Serving ideas:
  ◊ Use them in home remedies at the slightest sniffle. Add a spoonful of *amla* juice with honey, turmeric and pepper simmered in full-fat milk (fat is essential for the absorption of active ingredients in turmeric) for cough.

- **Nuts and seeds** as they provide healthy fats, zinc and calcium.
  Serving ideas:
  ◊ Nut butter spread on sandwiches, nuts caramelized with organic jaggery in salads or as a snack or trail mix.

- **Healthy carbohydrates** such as sweet potatoes as they provide beta carotene and fibre.
  Serving ideas:
  ◊ Bake the sweet potatoes and top them with pasta sauce and cheese.
  ◊ Slice the sweet potatoes and use them in place of nachos, topped with beans, salsa, grated cheese, mashed avocado, and herbs.
  ◊ Sweet potato fries made in a pan.

- Ensure that you provide **whole grain bread** like *rotis*, loaves or *parathas* to provide energy for their daily activities.

- **Omega-3 rich foods** such as flax seeds, chia seeds, walnuts and oily fish sources (such as salmon, tuna, mackerel, if fish are a part of the diet) are important as they benefit brain health[3]. They are also said to improve sleep[4], attention-deficit/hyperactivity disorder (ADHD), and symptoms of asthma.

  Serving ideas:

  ◊ Add ground flaxseeds to home-baked snacks like muffins, cakes, and bread.

  ◊ Ground flax seeds or flaxseed oil can also be added to smoothies or salad dressings.

  ◊ Ground walnuts can also be added to baked goods as well as dips like pesto and smoothies.

Amaranth hemp seed pesto (page 189)

Amla in brine (page 186)

Avocado pomelo salad (page 222)

Black-eyed peas, chargrilled corn and rocket salad (page 214)

Broccoli pakodis in kadhi (page 230)

Broccoli sesame seed pesto (page 188)

Cauliflower cabbage carrot kootu (page 241)

Coriander turmeric chutney (page 193)

Homemade kanji podi mix (page 194)

Millets in tomato sauce parcels (page 227)

Muhammara with greens *(page 197)*

Pineapple pomegranate yoghurt bowls *(page 211)*

Pomelo betel leaf salad
(page 224)

Red grapes and mung
sprouts salad (page 220)

Spiced smokey beans
(page 202)

Tamarind mint appetiser drink
(page 206)

6

Getting Practical with Superfoods

Superfood ready reckoner

Keep a copy of the superfoods list (Table 6.1) stuck on your fridge or kitchen cabinet and in your phone's notes. Use it for your grocery shopping, including at least some of these items every week, depending on whatever is in season. Even if you are not into planning menus, make sure to eat three to four items from this list every day. It is easy to include one of the grains for breakfast, one of the vegetables in a curry, one of the legumes in a lunch salad and one of the seeds or nuts in a snack.

Treat every meal and snack as an opportunity to add one or more superfoods to your daily diet.

Table 6.1: List of Superfoods

Grains	Amaranth
	Buckwheat
	Millets
Beans	Black-eyed peas
	Green moong
	Soybeans

Vegetables	Bell pepper
	Broccoli
	Cabbage
	Cauliflower
	Dark green leafy veg
	Moringa
	Onions
	Pumpkin
	Sweet potato
	Tomato
Fruits	*Amla*
	Avocado
	Dates
	Pineapple
	Pomegranate
	Pomelo
	Red grapes
	Strawberries
	Tamarind
	Watermelon
Spices, etc.	Black pepper
	Dark chocolate
	Garlic
	Ginger
	Nutmeg
	Turmeric

Nuts and seeds	Almonds, cashews, pistachios, walnuts
	Flax seeds
	Hemp seeds
	Sunflower seeds
Others	Green tea
	Mushrooms
	Wheatgrass

Weekly menu planning

Menu planning comes with a lot of benefits.

1. Time management – When you know the menu for the next day, the ingredients can be prepped, soaked and laid out whenever you have some free time or you are doing some other chores in the kitchen. This saves precious time when you have to cook.
2. Combining chores – While this is a part of time management, it is worth a separate mention. It saves a lot of time to combine common tasks, rather than doing them separately. As per your planned weekly menu, if you need dal for dinner and potatoes for breakfast, you can cook both in a pressure cooker in different compartments. This saves time, effort, and fuel. Get the mirepoix (carrot-onion-celery mix) for the soup chopped up and saved in an airtight box, when you use the food processor for some other dish during the day. Combining prep is possible only if we know what's planned for the next few meals.
3. Eating healthy balanced meals – An overview of a weekly menu can tell if there is enough protein, complex carbs, vegetables and fruits in the daily diet. Here are some pointers on planning a well-balanced menu. Proteins, more specifically the amino acids, are the building blocks of the body. Our body manufactures 11 out of 20 amino acids,

and the remaining nine need to be provided through your diet, which is why they are called essential amino acids. Except for soy and quinoa, all plant-based foods are incomplete proteins as they do not have all the essential amino acids. A combination of various plant-based and dairy foods such as grains, lentils, vegetables, milk products, etc., gives you all nine essential amino acids during the course of a day. Simple changes to your foods will ensure you get your optimum protein intake even if you are a vegetarian:

- Peanut butter or hummus instead of plain butter on toast.
- Milk or soy milk instead of water to prepare porridge.
- Paneer *bhurji* with roti.
- Combination of dal and rice in *khichdi, idlis* and dosas.
- Cheese and a few nuts, hard-boiled eggs or yoghurt to go along with an Indian meal or along with breakfast dishes like paratha or *upma*.

For vegetarians and vegans, it is good to plan such complete protein meals in the weekly menu.

While the quantity of carbohydrates in our diet is never a problem, it is the quality that matters. Whole grains over refined flours, whole lentils and beans, starchy vegetables, etc., are all easy ways to incorporate good carbohydrates in your menu plan.

There's a lot of confusion regarding fats. You cannot, however, go wrong if you stick to fats in moderation, using it to add flavour and satiety to a meal. A teaspoon of ghee in a dal rice meal or extra virgin olive oil in a salad dressing or coconut oil to temper a south Indian vegetable dish all help add flavour and enable absorption of fat-soluble vitamins like A, E, D, and K. Choose cold-pressed oils wherever possible.

Snacks are often highly processed foods out of a packet, made using refined flour, deep-fried or with added sugar, and most often containing no protein. Be conscious of consuming a small portion of protein as a part of your snacks too.

4. Getting kids involved – Ask kids to make a note of the dishes they would like to include in the weekly menu plan, which will make them take an active interest in eating healthy.
5. Kitchen economics – When buying vegetables and fruits online, it is easy to go overboard and buy too much. When we prepare a weekly menu and then go shop, it limits our buying to the things we need. This ensures that half the fresh stuff is not languishing at the bottom of the vegetable crisper. The other way to go about this is to ensure that you make the menu, keeping in mind the fridge and pantry items, on a first-in-first-out basis, or on the basis of the shelf life of the produce. For example, using up greens, lettuce and other delicate vegetables early on and leaving the root vegetables for later as they will stay for a couple of weeks.

While it is a bit time consuming initially, it does get easier and you can always repeat the same menu every few weeks.

Table 6.2: Weekly Menu Planning Table

	Mon	Tue	Wed	Thu	Fri	Sat	Sun
Breakfast							
Lunch							
Dinner							
Snacks							

How to incorporate superfoods in your menu

Now that the weekly menu is planned and ready, the next step is to see how superfoods can be seamlessly integrated into your daily meals.

As an exercise, list the most common dishes prepared in your home for breakfast, snacks, and main meals. Refer to the superfoods list (on page 149) and see how best you can fortify these dishes. Over a period of time, this will become second nature to you.

Table 6.3: Few Example Dishes with Ways to Make Them More Nutritious

Upma	Make it with any of the millets, with the addition of ginger, tomatoes, black pepper, and turmeric.
Tea / Coffee	Green tea, turmeric tea, or buttermilk with black pepper.
Alcoholic beverage	Wine comes loaded with more antioxidants than any other alcoholic drink. Drink in moderation though.
Sandwich for kids' snack	Nut butter or black-eyed peas hummus sandwich.
Fried starters	Steamed or roasted broccoli florets or carrot sticks, dipped in hung yoghurt dip or a hummus.
Paratha and pickle or raita	Amaranth paratha with instant turmeric pickle or *amla* raita.
Potato curry, dal and white polished rice	Sweet potato curry, tomato dal with turmeric and millet.

Lunch salad	Moong sprouts, a roasted garlic dressing topped with hemp seed hearts or chopped nuts.
Dessert	Dark chocolate and nut bark, fruit sorbets.

Taking an everyday meal to superfood meal level can be quite fun. You will even end up creating new flavours and new dishes in the process. This is the easiest and simplest way to ramp up the superfood component in your meal without much of a change in the menu.

Shopping for superfoods

Now that we have a superfood-rich menu planned for the week, it is easy to make a shopping list.

I would recommend that you buy fresh produce twice a week. In an unprocessed diet lifestyle, you will be eating a lot more fruits and vegetables so instead of stuffing up the fridge for an entire week, splitting up the fresh produce shopping for three to four days at one time is a practical approach. In-season produce is easy to identify by its abundance and price – you'll find it is much cheaper. Groceries can be bought fortnightly or monthly. Some ingredients such as ground turmeric and tamarind can be bought when in season and stocked up for the whole year in the fridge or freezer.

My next recommendation is to shop the rainbow. Whether it is vegetables, fruits, beans or grains, look to buy them in a variety of colours as they bring a whole range of phytonutrients to the table.

If you have kids at home, take them along for food shopping. It is a great way for them to learn how to pick fruits and vegetables. It is also good that they become interested in food shopping and healthy eating right from their early years.

When buying packaged food in the supermarket, always read the nutrition labels of the product to know the ingredients. Anything that claims to be whole grain must have that ingredient featured in the top one or two items on that list. In case you need to make a choice between brands, compare the nutrition labels to see what fares better. This is initially a time-consuming process, but soon you'll be a pro at it. If the nutrition label has too fine a print to read, use your phone camera to zoom in and read it.

It is alright to buy frozen, canned, pureéd or dried goods. Ensure that they are preservative-free and no added sugar has been used. Canned beans can be rinsed in water before use to get rid of excess sodium.

Where to shop:

1. **Local markets** – Most cities have their designated outdoor markets, for example, KR Market and HAL market in Bengaluru, where you have access to fresh seasonal produce.
2. **Farmers' markets** – More and more farmers markets are being organized in cities like Bengaluru, Mumbai and Chennai. These are held at specific locations on a certain day of the week. Look for such updates on social media and shop there to support local farmers.
3. **Local organic stores** – These stores stock essential groceries like rice and dal, cold-pressed oils, etc., sourced from local farmers in small batches. Shopping here indirectly helps the local farmers.
4. **Online shopping** – Ingredients like seeds, nuts, dried fruits, superfood powders, etc., can be bought online. Many states have NGO/cooperative run websites that sell local organic produce. For example, tonsvalley.shop sells locally grown organic walnuts, apples and rajma.

5. **Exhibitions** – In Bengaluru, there is a millet fair organized every year where hundreds of stalls sell local organic produce. The Mahalaxmi Saras held in many cities in India is another such exhibition selling artisanal food products, traditional cookware, etc.
6. **Direct from farmers** – Many enterprising farmers offer fresh produce from their farm directly to communities. This is especially true for mangoes during the mango season and also fruits from Himachal such as apples, persimmon and kiwis. Keep a lookout for such farmers on social media and organize for them to supply produce directly to your residential complex.

Safety in cooking and storage

Choosing the right cookware is as important as buying quality ingredients. There is a lot of confusion about which pans to cook in. Let us examine the choices we have and what material is best and safest for our health.

Non-stick

We have all used (or continue to use) non-stick cookware for its sheer convenience in cooking, ditching the old iron and other traditional pans passed down from the previous generations. I have used my fair share of non-stick pots and pans. It is a boon for flipping the perfect dosas without a care in the world, scrambling eggs, making curries with very little oil or ghee and the clean-up is a breeze too.

The synthetic coating that prevents food from sticking to the pan is polytetrafluoroethylene (PTFE), commonly known as Teflon. In the earlier days, another compound called perfluorooctanoic acid (PFOA) was used for the coating. This was believed to be a carcinogen, causing cancers of the thyroid, liver and testicles, and also causing kidney disorders. Unlike PFOA, Teflon has been found to be safe, although high-temperature cooking is not recommended even in Teflon-coated pans.

If you are ready to move away from non-stick pans, there are many better and safer options. But if you must use non-stick, make sure to follow these precautions:

1. Invest in a high quality brand that has a heavier pan. It must also have multiple layers of coating that make it more durable and the heavy pan prevents overheating.
2. Do not heat an empty pan. It can cause the compounds in the coating to be released as toxic fumes. Use non-stick pans to cook on low and medium heat.
3. Use wooden or silicone spatulas only so that the metal spoons don't scrape and break the coating layer.
4. Hand wash the pan gently using a soft, non-scratch scrubber.
5. Discard the pan when the non-stick pan surface starts flaking or losing its properties. Even the high-quality non-stick cookware has a lifespan of three to four years only.

If you are ready to give up on non-stick cookware, here are the preferred materials for cooking pots and pans. Some of these may be expensive, but they also last for generations.

Stainless steel

Stainless steel cookware is totally safe and long-lasting. These are also induction friendly as long as the utensil has a flat base. Ensure you look for the tri-ply variety as the thinner ones are not suitable for cooking. In lightweight stainless steel pans, food sticks to the pan and burns in no time. Look for stainless steel pressure cookers and pressure pans too. Do take note that stainless steel pressure cookers in bigger sizes can be quite heavy to lift, especially when loaded with food.

Cast iron

Used extensively by the previous generations, cast iron is making a big comeback due to its safety and durability. It retains heat and cooks the food evenly. Cooking food in cast iron pans adds to the iron content of the food. Its heavy weight and somewhat higher price may be a deterrent for some. However, the initial investment pays off as a cast iron pan is for life if taken care of properly. Cooking acidic dishes such as a tomato-based curry can turn the curry a shade of grey due to a reaction with the pan, but it is still safe to consume.

A seasoned cast iron pan almost behaves like a non-stick pan. These days, ready-to-use, pre-seasoned cast iron utensils are available, which can be cooked in right away. Wash cast iron with a gentle soap, then dry immediately and smear a thin layer of oil over the surface. A lot of locally made cast iron utensils are available both online and in shops in India. It makes sense to have a set of two cast iron pans in different sizes.

Soapstone

Soapstone is one of the earliest heat-resistant materials used for making cooking pots. We are seeing a revival of soapstone cookware (*kalchatti* in Tamil) in places like Chennai and Bengaluru. Soapstone has its origins as talc that combines with other minerals over time to result in a porous material. It feels slippery to touch, therefore the name 'soapstone'. It can be used over a flame or in the oven too. Stone pots retain heat for longer. Due to the slippery surface, it is easy to clean without much scrubbing. Cooking in soapstone utensils may improve iron levels[1] in adult women.

Clay pots

Clay pots can also be used for cooking. When buying a clay pot, look for an unglazed finish and go with trusted brands that use good quality materials with no added chemicals. Cooking in clay pots is said to add to the mineral content of the food by way of iron and calcium. Clay pots for cooking add their own rustic flavour to curries and more. Tamarind and citrus-based curries can be cooked in clay pots as the pots do not react with any acidic or alkaline foods. Biryanis can be finished in clay pots with the dough seal and baked in the oven.

Storing water in clay *matkas* is an age-old custom in many parts of India as well. One-litre capacity clay bottles with lids are available to store water.

Aluminum and anodized cookware

Aluminium cookware and anodized cookware are avoidable. Aluminium is a toxin for the nervous system and immune system. Cooking food in aluminium vessels or storing food in aluminium containers may leech some of the metal into the food. While anodized cookware is said to provide a protecting coating over the aluminium, repeated usage and washing may create breaks in the layer, leaving food exposed to aluminium in the long run. While only traces of aluminium may leech into food, it is better to consider the safer options given above.

Glass boxes for storage

Meal prep is one of the practical ways to everyday healthy eating. Prepped food needs to be stored in containers in optimum conditions in the refrigerator. For food storage, choose glass boxes with lids. Not only are these safer than plastic, but being see-through, it is easier to see the contents of these boxes in the refrigerator. Keep a stock of five to six glass boxes in various sizes. These can be used to store foods like cooked beans, brown rice, prepped vegetables, etc., and a few glass jars and bottles can be used to store dressings, chutneys and dips. These glass boxes can also be used to store leftovers in the fridge. It is convenient to pop these boxes in the microwave to reheat the leftovers as well. Avoid reheating food in plastic containers, especially the thin quality restaurant containers.

How safe is cling film?

Besides being environmentally damaging due to its single-use nature, it is best to not let cling film touch the surface of the food. Plastic is made up of a medley of chemicals, some of which may be harmful to human health when it comes in contact with food and in case there is a migration of chemicals to the food being heated. When microwaving food, take the same precautions, or cover the food loosely with a microwave-safe lid. Instead of using cling film to wrap leftover bits of vegetable, cheese or food in bowls to be refrigerated, use beeswax paper that is available in some online sustainable stores. These are 100 per cent natural and reusable.

Is aluminium foil safe?

Aluminium foil is a common feature in modern Indian kitchens, used to wrap rotis and parathas for lunch boxes or lining baking trays to prevent them from getting messy. Some aluminium does leach into food from containers, vessels or foil. The incidence of leaching increases with higher temperature, acidic ingredients in food and the presence of salt and certain spices. Dietary aluminium has been linked to Alzheimer's disease, and it is a good enough reason to keep our body's exposure to this metal to a bare minimum. While using foil once in a while is not going to lead to too much exposure, you must avoid using it at high heat, with sour ingredients or with salt and spices.

How to meal prep

Meal prep is a practical way to ensure that a healthy meal can be ready with minimum effort and time. Keeping some of the essential components of a balanced meal prepped and refrigerated enables us to rustle up something healthy even when we are short on time and energy.

Ingredients like brown rice, beans and dal take long to cook, so it makes sense to cook them in big batches so that they can be used for two to three meals. To make hearty salads, it helps to have a few things prepped and ready to go after which you just need to add a handful of everything to make a salad full of all the required nutrients.

Choose a free day of the week to shop and prep for the whole week. Here are some of the things that can be prepared and kept for use during the week:

- Instant breakfast mixes using a mix of flours, spices and tempering
- Batter for *idli*/dosa/*uthappam*
- Cooked potatoes, beets, sweet potatoes
- Toasted seeds
- Chutneys, dressings, dips
- Vegetables like radish, carrot, beets, bell peppers, cut into strips for snacks and salads
- Cauliflower, cleaned and grated, and saved in airtight bags in the fridge or freezer to make quick cauliflower rice
- Beans, soaked and cooked
- Beans, soaked and sprouted
- Dals, cooked and frozen in portions to make dal/soups
- Green leafy vegetables, blanched/puréed
- Hard-boiled eggs
- Red rice or unpolished rice, cooked
- Quinoa, millets, barley or amaranth, cooked
- Shelled pomegranate

Use glass boxes and jars to store all the prepped ingredients in the fridge with the more perishable ingredients to be used first kept in the front of the fridge. Almost all the recipes given in the chapter on basic recipes (page 186 onwards) are suitable for meal prep.

Superfood swaps

Here's a list providing superfood swaps, or just more nutritious options, for regular foods. It also includes local foods that can be used instead of imported superfoods.

Staple	Alternative
Polished white rice	Single polished rice or millet
Maida	Whole wheat flour
Sugar	Organic jaggery powder (more nutrients and fewer chemicals used in processing) or raw cane sugar
Cornflakes	Steel-cut oats
Pasta from refined flour	Whole wheat pasta, lentil pasta, zucchini
Ice cream	Blended frozen fruits
Fruit juice	Whole fruit
Mayonnaise	Hung yoghurt dressing
White sauce for pasta	Tomato-based sauce with herbs
Masala chai	Green tea
Quinoa	Millet
Blueberries	*Ber*, *amla*, *shahtoot*, pomegranate
Chia seeds	Basil seeds
Kale	Mustard greens, cauliflower, radish leaves
Milk chocolate	Dark chocolate

Create your own superfood recipes

You can create your own superfood recipes, be it for your own and your family's consumption or for your cafe, catering or any other health food business.

It is fairly easy to come up with formulas of combinations, depending on the season, availability and flavour pairings.

1. Smoothies – Use yoghurt or milk (dairy- or plant-based) as a base. To this, add any seasonal frozen fruits, soaked chia seeds, overnight oats, a handful of green leafy vegetables and a natural sweetener of choice if the fruits are not sweet enough.
2. Breakfast yoghurt bowls – These are really popular in breakfast menus in cafes around the world. They are extremely trendy on Instagram for their pretty looks. Build a bowl with thick yoghurt (dairy- or plant-based), toasted seeds, berries if available, crunchy grains and a fruit preserve that adds flavour, colour and acts as a natural sweetener.
3. Bars – Breakfast bars sold commercially usually have a lot of cheap fillers, sweeteners and additives. However, when made at home using all-natural and superfood ingredients, it becomes a great portable breakfast or a snack to carry along on a long day. Use a combination of grains such as rolled oats or popped amaranth, nuts, seeds, dried fruit, a superfood powder and plant-based protein powder, all bound together using melted natural jaggery.
4. Porridge mix – Use a mix of grains, lentils and nuts and toast all of them until aromatic. Grind them into flour and stock the flour in an airtight container. This makes for a robust porridge mix. Whisk two to three tablespoons of the porridge mix in cold water. Add some more water and bring it to a simmer, cooking it for three to four minutes. Add a splash of milk (dairy- or plant-based), a natural sweetener of choice and have it while it's still hot.
5. Pancake/waffle mix – Use ingredients like buckwheat flour, amaranth flour, green moong flour, ground cinnamon, ground flaxseeds and ground almonds to fortify plain

flour to get a healthy pancake flour mix. Store this in the refrigerator, as flaxseed flour and almond flour have the tendency to go rancid at higher room temperatures. Desiccated coconut can also be added to the mix if its flavour is preferred. Make a batter using eggs, milk, butter or ghee and a natural sweetener to make pancakes or waffles. Top the cooked pancakes or waffles with chopped seasonal fruit. You can also try baking brownies, cookies and muffins using this flour blend.

6. Granola/cereal blend – Supermarkets and gourmet food stores are stuffed with aisles full of fancy cereals and granolas. The truth is that it is very easy to make your own blends, and superfood-rich ones at that. Choose a couple of grain options from popped amaranth, crispy toasted rolled oats, puffed rice, toasted quinoa or puffed jowar (sorghum). Add a mix of roughly chopped nuts, well-toasted seeds like sesame, flax, poppy, sunflower, watermelon or pumpkin and dried fruit such as raisins, cranberries, kiwi, papaya, pineapple. To this, add spices such as ground cinnamon or nutmeg for flavour. Coat all the ingredients with a natural sweetener like melted jaggery and toast the entire lot in the oven until golden and crunchy. Save this blend in an airtight bottle or container. These blends also make excellent edible gifts.
7. Energy balls – These recipes are quite the rage on the internet. They are a bite-sized, concentrated source of healthy fats and energy-boosting nutrients. Use a combination of nut butter, seeds, pureed or finely chopped dates and coarsely chopped nuts, and roll these mixed ingredients into balls. Dip them in melted dark chocolate ganache for a more decadent treat.
8. Soup – A soup which has whole grains, protein, fats and micronutrients is fit to be a one-pot meal, especially for dinners on cold days. Tomatoes along with any other

seasonal vegetables, aromatics like onion, garlic, celery and lentils, fillers like handmade pasta using chickpea flour, a whole grain like red rice, spices and herbs to suit your liking can be made into soups.

9. Burgers – Beans make the perfect base for a plant-based burger. Choose a combination of cooked mashed beans, a starchy vegetable, any other seasonal vegetables, herbs, spices, nuts and seeds to build your superfood burger. Choose from sweet potatoes or grated cooked beets, grated tofu, spices, herbs, sourdough breadcrumbs, almond meal and flaxseed meal to add to your burger. Serve with lettuce and sliced tomatoes.
10. Trail mix – Trail mixes are a handy, healthy and delicious thing to carry on long flights (if you are not a fan of in-flight dining), on treks and for children's school outings when they have to carry something dry and calorie-filled. Buy a variety of nuts, seeds and dried fruits. Toss the nuts and seeds in coarse salt and a natural sweetener like honey. Bake the mix in the oven until it is golden brown and crisp. Combine this with a mix of dried fruits. Large-sized dried fruits like apricot or dates can be chopped into smaller, bite-sized pieces. Pack the trail mix in resealable bags or airtight glass containers.
11. Tea blend – Tea blends are gaining popularity. Flavoured with flowers, herbs, spices, etc., there is no end to flavour combinations for a tea blend. Use dried *moringa* leaves, green tea, dried edible flowers and dried herbs. Choose from spices such as fennel, cinnamon, cloves, star anise, cardamom and dried ginger. Brew tea from this blend to sip through the day as a zero-calorie drink which also has health benefits. Just a note of caution – some people may be allergic or intolerant to certain herbs and flowers, so please use only those botanicals whose safety you are sure of.

12. Latte – What's better than a soothing nightcap to end the day! Make your superfood-rich latte mix with the addition of dark cocoa powder, turmeric, ground cinnamon or ground almonds. Mix in a couple of tablespoons into hot milk or any non-dairy milk and sweeten it with a natural sweetener.

Superfoods in your lunch box

Invest in good quality lunch boxes. Plastic boxes are not good to pack hot food and also don't last for long. Regularly replacing the old boxes with new adds to the plastic waste in the environment. Steel thermos-like containers, while expensive, will last longer, are food safe and environmentally friendly. Consider buying a thermos-type box for hot soups, pasta, curries, etc. Use refillable steel water bottles. Avoid single-use cling film to wrap food. Reusable beeswax wraps are a better alternative in terms of sustainability, zero waste, and safety.

Children's lunch boxes need to be packed with more complex carbs to fuel their physical activity and sports in school as well as after school. Adult lunch boxes can be made as per dietary preferences and any specific nutritional needs.

A lunch box must be a smaller version of a full meal we have at home, i.e., balanced in proteins, carbohydrates and fats. Make sure that the food you pack in your lunch box has a hearty dose of superfoods.

For example, each of these items includes at least one superfood:

- Millet *idlis* with lentil and flaxseed *podi*
- Sesame rice with yoghurt
- Buckwheat noodles or pasta in tomato sauce
- Apple, paneer (or cheese) and nut butter sandwiches
- DGLVs made into a green sauce for pasta or curry
- Baked sweet potato with tomato sauce

- Sprouts and vegetable salad
- Bean salad with bell peppers
- Roasted broccoli with hummus and pita
- Sprouts chaat
- Sweet potato salad
- Pomegranate/red grapes/dark chocolate as a snack

Superfood snacks

There are times in the day when a sudden hunger pang strikes and we impulsively reach out for the first thing we lay our eyes on. Mostly, this is something out of a packet. To avoid such situations from springing up in our day, it is always a good idea to be well prepared with a few healthy alternatives. Be it at home, in the office, or stuck in long traffic jams on the way home in the evenings, such snacks come to the rescue:

- Chopped fruit or easy-to-eat fruit like grapes in a box
- Small portions of trail mix made from toasted seeds, nuts, grains and dried fruit
- Dark chocolate squares
- Salt and turmeric popcorn
- Herbal tea bags and hot water
- Toasted flaxseeds tossed in salt and spices
- Gujarati-style thin *methi theplas* (for long road trips or airplane food)
- Stock a couple of dips such as hummus and hung yoghurt in the refrigerator at home. Pair these with seeded crackers or veggie sticks. Slices of apple with peanut butter or any other nut butter also work well.

Superfood powders

Taking a mix of superfood powders in small doses is an easy way to gain all the benefits of eating superfoods, especially if you don't have the time to cook your meals or if you are eating on the go. They are available either in capsule form or in powder form. The powdered form can be mixed into smoothies or along with other foods. Some superfoods like spirulina and chlorella are difficult to have as part of a meal so these are best had in powder form. Given that even when we consciously cook all our meals at home, we fail to include enough fruits and vegetables, this is a clever fix to make up for the lack of nutrients. If the superfoods from which the powders are made are organic, it makes it easier for us to have a steady supply of organic superfoods as part of our diet.

As long as there are no additives and the nutrition label shows that it has only one ingredient, the powders have all the health benefits of the fresh version of the superfood. The advantage is that these powders are available all year round. The fresh produce is seasonal and even when it is in season, it may not be possible to stock up on them all the time.

Some of these powders are expensive as they are grown organically, under optimum conditions for the best nutritional profile, while also offering a fair price to the farmers. These higher prices can be considered as an investment towards our health.

The best way to eat supplements – or in this case superfood powders – is along with a meal, so the body absorbs it better. Having supplements with breakfast is a good idea.

Here are some commonly used superfood powders:

1. *Moringa* powder can be used in smoothies, bakes, soup and oats porridge. It is rich in vitamin A, calcium, iron, potassium and fibre.
2. Spirulina powder is obtained from algae and it is rich in antioxidants, essential amino acids and protein. Add it to smoothie bowls, soups and spinach-based dishes like *palak paneer*.
3. Alfalfa is grown as animal feed. It belongs to the legume family. The leaves are dried and ground to a powder for human consumption. It is protein-rich and a good source

of vitamins, minerals, calcium and iron. It has cholesterol-lowering properties due to fibre and saponins and also has anti-inflammatory properties useful in asthma and arthritis.

4. Chlorella is another alga like spirulina. It is a complete protein source with all the essential amino acids. It is rich in iron and vitamin C, which helps the body absorb the iron better. Just three grams of chlorella gives 100 milligram of omega 3. It is also rich in the carotenoids lutein and zeaxanthin, making it excellent for eye health.

Superfood shopping on your travels

I remember eating kilos of mangosteen and rambutan when travelling in Malaysia. Besides enjoying local fruits and vegetables on my travels, I also love bringing back local foods as souvenirs—be it varieties of noodles from Hong Kong, local rice and cheese from Sikkim, or spice mixes from Mauritius. These cost much less in their place of origin as compared to buying them with all the duties and taxes built-in at the airport or when they are imported. Enjoy local superfoods as a snack or a meal while travelling to different places.

What to buy?

1. Buy local superfoods from supermarkets or farmers' markets. For example, the Borough Market in London has dozens of people selling artisanal food. A lot of unusual spices and ingredients can be found here.
2. Buy seeds to grow local plants of the place you are visiting in your garden back home, but do take care of the weather conditions these plants require. Buying seeds can usually be done within the country as purchasing and bringing in seeds from other countries may not be allowed.
3. It is safe to buy and bring back dried ingredients like mushrooms, dried fruits, nuts, and sundried foods that have a longer shelf life.

4. Local spices from different regions within India bring a multitude of flavours into your kitchen. Spices can also last longer if they are kept in airtight bags in the freezer.
5. Preserves, pickles, tea, and coffee are also good souvenirs to get.

Setting up a kitchen garden

A kitchen garden or a windowsill garden is a source of much joy. It can yield little or lots of produce fresh for the plucking. If you have a small space for a garden, then I strongly recommend that you use it as an edible garden as against just a landscaped one. With some thought put into them, edible gardens can look as pretty, if not prettier than a landscaped garden and give year-round gifts.

Ever since I invested time and effort in a small kitchen garden, every day has been a learning experience. For example, while growing cauliflower as well as broccoli, I saw how cauliflowers grow on the surface of the soil, while broccoli grows nearly two feet off the ground. This is probably why broccoli is hardly infested with worms. I learnt that leaves from the pumpkin vine and sweet potato creepers are edible. I learnt how delicious onion flowers are, and how invasive mint is.

At one point, I learnt how to channelize my frustration with a lemon bush that did not fruit for years. Providing it with optimum nutrients, moving its position to face the sun, spraying honey water to increase the chances of bee pollination – all of these actions coaxed the bush into giving out more flowers, which led to more fruits. Once the fruits appeared, it took around three to four weeks to ripen and attain its maximum size. All this made me think that a measly ₹5 is too little to pay for a lemon. When we see the kind of problems encountered and the patience required to grow any crop, we feel a renewed sense of respect for the farmers.

It made me wonder about the bunch of curry leaves, coriander, ginger and chilli that we expect to be given complimentary when we buy a big bag of vegetables. When we grow these ourselves, we realize how much effort goes into these so-called freebie vegetables and herbs.

Setting up a kitchen garden allows you to experience the other edible parts of a plant that never make their way into shops or markets, such as pumpkin leaves, sweet potato leaves, onion flowers, and carrot and radish leaves. Edible flowers of various vegetables can add colour and beauty to salads. Most of these secondary edible parts are full of flavour and as nutritious or sometimes more than the commonly used primary parts.

Produce like green chillies, curry leaves, coriander, basil, thyme, spinach, and lettuce have a different level of freshness and flavour when plucked and used immediately in dishes. All of these can be easily grown in pots as long as you have access to a sunny windowsill.

Tips for growing your own grub

1. Start with good quality soil. For most kitchen gardening, a mix of garden soil, compost and cocopeat in a 1:1:1 ratio will work.
2. Convert all your kitchen wet waste into compost. Read up or watch YouTube videos on home composting. There are plenty of avid gardeners from India and around the world who are generously sharing their knowledge on the internet.
3. Avoid monoculture. Even if you have a 9 sq feet piece of land, plant five or more different plants in this square. This ensures that a single pest cannot ruin the whole square.
4. Companion plants protect each other from pests. For example, basil and celery can be grown with tomato, radish with lettuce and marigold with brinjal.
5. Keep rotating the planting. Do not plant a vegetable in the same spot year after year.

6. Learn how to manage pests the organic way.
7. Join local kitchen gardening groups on Facebook where people exchange knowledge and tips, provide inspiration and help you solve your gardening problems.

To start with, all kinds of herbs and green leafy vegetables can be grown on a small patch of land or in pots on a windowsill. Vines like Malabar spinach grow beautiful shiny leaves that can cover an old window grill or climb up any available trellis in the garden. Yard long beans also climb up available spaces, providing green cover and a regular supply of beans.

If you live in an apartment, the residents can make the joint decision of growing a few *moringa* trees, *amla* trees, pomegranate trees, avocado trees and lime bushes along the compound wall, such that all the residents can get their share of homegrown superfood produce. Fruit trees take time to give yield but once they begin, they are bountiful year after year.

A corner patch enriched with well-rotted compost can be used to grow root vegetables like sweet potatoes, which take off rapidly once sown. A community gardener can be hired using pooled resources. The children living in the apartment complex should be involved in the process so that they get a first-hand understanding of how food is grown. In fact, every residential community should have a small organic gardening committee that ensures that any free space can be used productively to grow food.

There are plenty of resources in the form of websites, YouTube channels and books to learn the basics of organic kitchen gardening. It is a life skill that is sure to contribute greatly in your pursuit of good health and well-being.

There is a welcome trend of renting farmland, which is tended to by farmers and from which the fresh produce either gets delivered to the home of the person renting the farmland or the individual goes to the farmland over the weekend and gets their produce home. These kinds of farms are coming up in the outskirts of most cities. It is a prospect worth investing in if it seems exciting to you. City-based restaurants are also starting to take the farm-to-table concept seriously. When they practice this, not only is the quality of produce going into their dishes assured, thereby giving a consistently good taste, but they are also respecting their diners by cooking with the best of ingredients.

Restaurants like 'The Farm' in Chennai take pride in growing most of their produce locally and in serving the customer with almost zero food miles and carbon footprint.

Farm visits to understand food

Given our tight urban spaces and busy schedules, a kitchen garden is not an easy possibility for everyone. Most city-bred kids do not get a chance to see where their food comes from. If you live in a city, food is usually something you get from a supermarket or online stores. We do not have the time or inclination to dig deeper into the provenance of our food and this is understandable. However, it is important to take baby steps towards understanding more about the food we eat.

A good way to get familiar with the origins of the food we eat is to take out time and make trips with the entire family to nearby farms. This allows us to be one with nature, and to look at fruits and vegetables in their natural settings. This is a great learning experience for children and adults alike. We are fortunate to have many such farms in the outskirts of our cities. Many of these farms can be found online, and you can call or email the farmers and schedule a visit. Many farms also have a visit and pluck session when a fruit like mango is in season.

A lot of modern farmers take such familiarization sessions for school children and families, allowing them to experience a day in the life of a farmer. In these sessions, participants are involved in tasks such as preparing the soil, sowing seeds, weeding, harvesting and more. It is an opportunity for kids to develop a better appreciation of food and an understanding of nature and its elements. They get to know how food grows, the factors that affect growing cycles along with lessons of problem-solving, developing patience, etc. These farm visits should be a regular feature and not just once a year, so the children can see the crops in various stages of their life cycle, and in different seasons.

7

Superfoods and Sustainability

What is food sustainability?

Food sustainability is the ability to produce enough food to sustain the human population. It is impacted by many factors like the availability of suitable land, climatic conditions, soil fertility, water consumption, the usage of fertilizers, and human factors such as the choice of diet, the food supply chain, food wastage, etc. In short, sustainable food depends on how the food is grown, packaged, distributed, and consumed.

If you plan to change your food habits for life, your choices need to be sustainable. You should not only avoid fads, but also imported environment-damaging ingredients. Sustainable farming practices that tread gently on the environment, regard for animal welfare and fair working conditions for employees are a few of the other things to think about when you choose your superfoods. Of course, the choices also depend on your dietary preferences, convenience and budget.

What are the most sustainable diets?

Reducing meat consumption and increasing plant-based consumption is said to have the least impact on the environment and thereby is most sustainable. A 2010 report by the UNFAO, titled, 'Sustainable Diets and Biodiversity' stated that, 'sustainable diets are those diets with low environmental impacts which contribute to food and nutrition security and to healthy life for present and future generations. Sustainable diets are protective and respectful of biodiversity and ecosystems, culturally acceptable, accessible, economically fair and affordable, nutritionally adequate, safe and healthy, while optimizing natural and human resources'.

While vegan food is most ethical to animals, it may not be the most sustainable of all diets. As per research, a vegan diet leaves a lot of resources unused, such as land that is only usable as a pasture for grazing and not for growing crops[1]. Many crops used regularly in a vegan diet, such as soybeans, are not always grown sustainably[2]. Almond milk, which is used as a dairy milk substitute, is notorious for its water footprint. One litre of almond milk requires over 6,000 litres of water[3]. A study on food sustainability involving researchers from six universities in the US found vegetarianism, more specifically lacto-vegetarianism, as the most sustainable of all diets – providing sufficient nutrition to the entire population.

A superfood-rich diet may also pose problems for the farmers and the environment, similar to how the quinoa situation developed in South America (described later in the chapter). 'Trending' superfoods such as avocado, turmeric, kale, etc., command a higher market value for farmers and retailers, which leads to monocropping. Monocropping is growing only one kind of crop, without any crop rotation. This depletes soil quality forcing the farmers to use fertilizers and pesticides, which further worsens the soil and affects the groundwater. While it may give temporary higher returns to the farmers, this is not a sustainable farming method.

The quinoa story

Quinoa is a high-protein, high-fibre seed (treated as a grain) and one of the few vegetarian foods that is a complete protein because of the presence of all nine essential amino acids. It is also rich in vitamins and minerals.

It is a plant native to Central and South America, originating in Peru and Bolivia. It was domesticated in South America between 5000 and 3000 BCE. The first exports to the US began in 1984, after which it slowly started getting international attention. A local crop that was mainly grown for domestic consumption with hardly any commercial value was suddenly gaining global limelight. Between 2000 to 2008, the price of quinoa increased by a whopping 600 per cent because of its rising popularity in the US, Europe and Australia. Such was its craze that the year 2013 was declared as the International Year of Quinoa by the United Nations General Assembly. A small-scale manually grown crop turned into a crop grown by large-scale mechanized farming.

As quinoa started commanding a lucrative price in other parts of the world, all of it was kept aside to be sold while the local farmers in South America traded their quinoa-based diets for more non-traditional foods like rice and pasta. Farmers also began to use all the available land to grow one kind of quinoa that had the most demand in the market which led to monocropping that threatened biodiversity. This along with rapid scaling up of quinoa production also affected soil quality[4].

Over the last few years, quinoa production has moved into other parts of the world. By 2017, quinoa was being grown in 50 countries around the world, including India. This explains why the cost of quinoa has come down in India from around ₹3,000 a kilo from 5–6 years ago to ₹290 a kilo in 2020.

Quinoa being a rain-fed crop grows well in the semi-arid regions of India during winters. Rice needs nearly 3,000–6,000 litres of water to produce one kilo as against quinoa that needs 500 litres of water. The quinoa grown locally is possibly a more sustainable option than rice, given its shorter growing period and low water requirement. It is, of course, a more expensive food and not feasible as a staple for most of us due to very small quantities being grown locally as compared to the traditional Indian grains.

Cast a wider net to include more biodiverse produce

Sustainability can be achieved by making full use of the edible plant species that grow naturally in our region. Nature provides us with an immense variety of foods to enjoy a lifelong healthy diet. Here are some mind-boggling numbers from the book *Cultivated Plants, Primarily as Food Sources* by György Füleky:

- Total number of plant species – 3,91,000.
- 2,000 new species are described every year.
- Out of this, 80,000 edible species are available to us.
- The number of species cultivated for human food or animal feed is a mere 150.
- Out of 150 cultivated species, just 30 species contribute to 95 per cent of a person's caloric intake.
- Half of our food is dependent on just four species – rice, maize, wheat and potato.

The huge disparity between the number of edible species available and the number of species actually consumed is thought-provoking.

To give you an idea as to the variety of foods available in India, take a look at the website for the Envis Centre on Medicinal Plants (http://envis.frlht.org/). It has a vast database of edible plants and a valuable search function. When you type *keerai* (greens in Tamil) in the vernacular search box, you get 23 varieties of *keerai* in the results. Type water amaranth/*ponnanganni keerai* in the search and it reveals that this leafy green vegetable has 112 vernacular names in Tamil alone! This gives us an idea of the extent to which it is used in the region, to be known by 100 different names.

Over the years, our selective consumption of produce and the exclusive reliance on supermarkets in urban areas for their supply has ensured that a very predictable and limited variety is made available to us. Compare the number of green leafy vegetables in the green section of a large supermarket versus on a small pushcart of a local vegetable vendor. You will find at least three times the variety in the latter.

Supermarket-driven eating habits restrict us to eat only the primary part of the plant. Take for example a radish or carrot – the roots of these vegetables are the primary edible part which are stocked in the shelves while the greens are discarded as they have a much shorter shelf life. Eating the secondary parts of the plant – which is popularly known as root to stem eating – is the more sustainable as well as a healthier way to eat.

As mentioned earlier, NUS is a term coined by UNFAO. Ranging from local beans, greens and grains to less popular vegetables, most of these foods are concentrated sources of nutrients. NUS foods have been domesticated by our ancestors for food, fodder, oil, medicinal purposes and more. Over the years, they have been forgotten with a focus on a select few popular plants.

Going back to eating a variety of foods like our ancestors also encourages a more diverse growing pattern. Not growing and consuming NUS leads to losing out on thousands of highly nutritious, easy-to-grow local foods. It is also a huge loss to the biological diversity of an area, which has an impact on soil health.

Relying on this wider species of plants for our daily calories will lead to less industrialized and commercial production of these crops and a more local-seasonal, farmer-centric approach to crops. This will be possible if more people take an avid interest in the provenance of food that is reaching their table.

Using NUS foods in our meals is a more sustainable way to seamlessly include nutrient-dense foods in our diet, be it via the traditional recipes or more modern adaptations of the same. To make the NUS produce more acceptable to our current palates, we can use them to make popular local dishes as well as dishes from international cuisines. For example:

- Locally foraged greens can be mixed into spinach to make a popular dish like palak paneer or mashed along with potatoes to make aloo *tikki.*
- Lesser-known tubers like *siru kizhangu* (Chinese potatoes) can be used to make oven-roasted wedges.
- Local seasonal fruits can be chopped and added to a salad or added to a fruit and vegetable juice.

One way to bring back these lesser-used foods into our daily diets is to reclaim free land around us for creating food forests, which should be a focussed government initiative. By this method, we can tackle urban afforestation, food security and sustainability all in one go, making immense positive changes to the environment around us.

Apartment complexes in cities can use up beds reserved for landscaping to create edible gardens, some of them including the NUS. The soil can be enriched with compost produced from the apartment kitchens' wet waste. The beds can be used to grow a number of herbs, shrubs, medicinal plants and trees that are feasible in the available area and the given climatic conditions. Rainwater harvesting can be employed to preserve rainwater for future use for the plants as well. This is a long-term plan but a simple and effective effort to ensure that our superfoods are plentiful and accessible. New apartment complexes should have these food-growing zones built into their initial plans.

Reducing food wastage

Food wastage happens at every stage from production to domestic consumption. In the production stage, food waste happens due to pest attacks and damage during harvesting; inadequate transportation and storage are some of the other reasons for food wastage during this phase. Food that remains unsold or uneaten and, thus, becomes spoiled is a form of food wastage that happens during the consumption phase. According to UNFAO, about one-third of all food produced for human consumption in the world is never eaten. By category, this includes 45 per cent of all fruit and vegetables, 35 per cent of fish and seafood, 30 per cent of cereals, 20 per cent of dairy products, and 20 per cent of meat.

Food loss, as reported by UNFAO in the Food Loss Index (FLI), occurs from post-harvest up to, but not including, the retail level.

There is a big environmental impact when food waste happens at the production level because of the loss of energy and natural resources used in growing the crop and associated greenhouse gas (GHG) emissions. When it happens at the consumption end, it is food that could have fed millions of hungry people in the world.

While in developed countries, the waste produced is more at a domestic level, in the developing/poorer countries, it is more at the production level. According to the Food Sustainability Index 2017[5], the countries with the lowest food waste generation per capita include Greece and China (44 kg per year), followed by India (51 kg). The countries with the highest waste creation are Australia (361 kg), followed by the USA (278 kg). According to UNFAO, if food waste were a country, it would be the one with the third-largest carbon footprint.

Preventing food loss at the production level needs government and state-level initiatives powered by science and technology. At the domestic/end-user level, a variety of conscious efforts such as community refrigerators to cater to the underprivileged, home composting units, pick-up of excess food from events and restaurants and distributing it to the needy, making use of less than perfect produce from the supermarkets, etc., can be done.

Tips to be a conscious consumer

Thinking about all-round sustainability in our food choices can be quite overwhelming. The process of making the right and sustainable choice in terms of food should not drive you to anxiety. The best way is to pick out the option that is feasible as well as environmentally sustainable in the long run. Here are a few tips to be a conscious consumer:

- Be aware of where the food comes from and how it is grown.
- Support local shops that are a short walk or cycle ride away. This prevents us from driving to shop for our essentials.
- Reject food items packed in single-use plastic, such as oranges and pomelos packed in cling wrap. Stripping off nature's protective packaging only to wrap it in plastic that will further pollute the environment is a terrible idea.
- While going out shopping, take along a few cloth bags or baskets depending on your shopping list. Cloth bags with inbuilt compartments are very useful to buy smaller

vegetables like beans, chillies, ladyfingers, etc., which otherwise get mixed up due to their size.

- Plan for the week and buy only as much food as is required to avoid food wastage. Same goes with ordering in or takeaway from a restaurant. Encourage restaurants and businesses that support eco-friendly packaging or allow bringing your own containers from home.
- Grow whatever is possible in pots in your own home garden or community gardens. Even if you grow one plant, like coriander or chilli, it contributes to food production in the world. Growing your own produce teaches you to the value of food as well.
- Invest in quality cookware like cast iron or steel which will last for decades, instead of non-stick that needs to be replaced often.
- Reduce, reuse and recycle diligently wherever possible.

Food miles and carbon footprint

A food's carbon footprint depends on the distance it travels from farm to plate. This is also referred to as food miles. Any food product also has a carbon cost which is the cost of its production and transportation. In food transportation, the mode of transport is an important factor – air transport being the one with the highest carbon footprint and shipping being the least.

As explained in a Harvard University article[6], 'Do food miles really matter?', a standard U.S. diet due to its high meat consumption has a higher carbon cost in production as compared to transportation. Therefore, the best way to reduce carbon footprint is to reduce the consumption of animal products. On the other hand, for vegan foods, the carbon cost from transportation is much higher than the cost of production, which makes it more viable to stick to more locally grown produce.

Locally grown produce may also not be the best option always. This is especially true when cold-weather foods are grown in tropical countries or tropical produce in cold countries since there is an added burden of providing hot or cold conditions that require tremendous energy. Thus, even though it is difficult to choose food purchases keeping all these factors in mind, it is good to be aware of these concepts.

DC Ram Singh, an IAS officer in Meghalaya, paints an inspiring picture in his social media posts. One of his photos from a weekend shopping trip has the caption *'21 kgs of weekend organic vegetable shopping. No plastic, no vehicular pollution, no traffic jam, 10km morning walk.'* He walks 10 kilometres to his local market to buy fruits and vegetables with a bamboo basket slung from his shoulders[7].

There's a lot to learn from the North-Eastern states of India when it comes to food management. Leaf packaging is very common for both cooked food and for produce. Most of the produce grown and sold in the open-air markets is organic. The produce sold is also hyper-local.

8

Everyday Superfood Recipes

MEAL PREP

AMLA IN BRINE

This is the easiest way to preserve *amla* or Indian gooseberries when they are in season and use them all year long. Soaked in brine, the tart *amla* gets an added salty flavour, which makes it a welcome addition to salads and *raitas.*

Ingredients

250 grams *amla* (10–11 medium-sized *amlas*)
1 tsp turmeric
2 tsp salt

Choose uniformly sized *amlas*. Wash and dry the *amlas* well.

Place the *amlas* in a pressure cooker and add enough water to cover them. Add the salt and turmeric to the water. Keep the flame on high and shut the lid of the pressure cooker. When the pressure builds up towards the first whistle, turn off the flame and open the cooker after five minutes by manually releasing the pressure. This ensures that the *amlas* do not overcook. In the cooking process, the *amlas* may separate into segments revealing the seed inside, and this is alright.

Remove the *amlas* and preserve in an airtight container, ensuring that the *amlas* are covered with the cooking liquid and not exposed to air.

Any remaining cooking liquid can be used to make *amla rasam* by addition of dal, spices and tempering.

How to use:

Grind a few *amlas* with green chillies and coconut. Add to whisked yoghurt to make a *raita*.

Toss with cucumber, onions, lettuce and extra virgin olive oil to make a salad.

Toss in mustard oil and instant pickling spice mix to make a pickle.

GINGER-GARLIC-TURMERIC-BLACK PEPPER CURRY PASTE

Ginger-garlic paste gives many Indian curries its oomph and flavour. This paste is superfood-charged with the addition of turmeric and black pepper. The compound piperine in black pepper enhances the absorption of curcumin, which is the active compound in turmeric, making it a total winner for our health.

Makes ½ cup

Ingredients

¼ cup peeled garlic cloves
¼ cup peeled and chopped ginger
2 tbsp peeled and chopped fresh turmeric
10–12 black peppercorns
1 tsp rock salt
1 tbsp vegetable oil

Method

Grind all the ingredients except the oil to a fine paste without any addition of water. Keep the paste in a clean and dry airtight glass jar topped with a layer of cooking oil.

How to use:

While preparing any curry using vegetables, paneer or meat, sauté one to two tablespoons of this paste in oil (depending on the quantity of the curry) and then proceed with the rest of the curry recipe. You can add tomato-onion paste to the sautéing process depending on what type of curry you are making.

Do note that the curry paste has some salt in it so adjust the salt in the dish accordingly.

BROCCOLI AND SESAME SEED PESTO

Try this recipe in winters when broccoli is in season and very fresh. It is a fun way to enjoy this superfood vegetable.

Makes 2 servings

Ingredients

2 cups medium-sized broccoli florets
2 tbsp sesame seeds
2 tbsp cashew nuts
4–5 cloves garlic
½ tsp salt
Zest of 1 lime
Juice of ½ lime
2 tbsp extra virgin olive oil

Method

Wash and steam the broccoli florets for four minutes in a covered microwave-safe bowl. You can also steam the florets in a stovetop steamer for five to six minutes.

Remove, drain and pat dry.

In a small pan, lightly toast the sesame seeds and cashew nuts together. The sesame seeds will start spluttering. Once the spluttering stops, remove to a dish and cool.

In a blender, combine garlic, the toasted sesame seeds and cashew nuts, salt, lime zest, lime juice and one tablespoon of the extra virgin olive oil. Blend to a coarse puree.

Add the steamed broccoli florets to the mix and process using the pulse function to get a coarse pesto. Pour in the remaining oil and pulse two to three more times for a few seconds each.

Remove to a glass jar and save in the refrigerator for up to one week.

How to use:

Use as a spread on sandwiches.
Serve as a dip for crackers.

Use as a pizza sauce.
Toss pasta in the pesto, thinned with some extra virgin olive oil.
Add it to a salad bowl.

AMARANTH AND HEMP SEED PESTO

This recipe makes use of a local green leafy vegetable along with hemp seeds from Uttarakhand to make a uniquely Indian pesto.

Makes 1 cup

Ingredients
3 cups green amaranth leaves
2 cloves garlic, peeled
3 tbsp *dalia* (fried gram)
2 tbsp hemp seeds, toasted
¼ tsp red chilli flakes
2 tbsp extra virgin olive oil
½ tsp salt

Method
Wash the leaves in plenty of water until no trace of mud remains.

For this recipe, use only the leaves and not the stems. The stems can be added to a dal or *sambar*.

Steam the leaves for three minutes in a covered microwave-safe bowl or in a stovetop steamer for four to five minutes. Remove and drain any excess water.

In a food processor, grind the garlic, *dalia*, hemp seeds, chilli flakes, half the oil and salt to a coarse paste.

To the paste, add the steamed amaranth leaves. Process by using the pulse function for a few seconds each time until the entire mix is a fine paste.

Save this in an airtight glass jar, top with remaining oil and store in the refrigerator for up to one week.

How to use:
Toss cooked pasta in this pesto.
Use this pesto to top baked potatoes or sweet potatoes.

TOASTED NUTS AND SEEDS TOPPING (TNST)

Once you prepare this nut and seed mix, you'll find yourself using it over everything. It adds a wonderful textural element to any dish, bringing along a dose of healthy fats.

Makes 2 cups

Ingredients

¼ cup sunflower seeds
¼ cup melon seeds
¼ cup pumpkin seeds
¼ cup flax seeds
¼ cup chopped walnuts
¼ cup chopped almonds
¼ cup white sesame seeds
¼ cup black sesame seeds

Method

Mix all the ingredients, except the two kinds of sesame seeds, in a bowl.

Heat a cast iron pan or any heavy-bottomed pan over a low flame. Stir the mixed nuts and seeds for 10–12 minutes until they turn aromatic and you can see them turn a shade darker.

At this point, add the sesame seeds and keep sautéing along with the other ingredients. The sesame seeds will start popping rapidly. Once the popping sounds stop, turn off the flame. Remove the mix on to a big tray or plate and allow it to come to room temperature.

Pack in an airtight bottle and keep refrigerated.

How to use:

Add TNST to a bowl of yoghurt with fresh fruits or fruit preserve.

Garnish a bowl of soup with TNST and microgreens.

Add to mashed avocado on toast, topped with a soft-boiled egg.

Sprinkle on top of peanut butter on toast, topped with sliced banana and honey.

Add TNST over a mixed greens salad.
Sprinkle TNST over broth and noodles.
Toss mini *idlis/dhoklas* in TNST.

ROASTED RED GRAPES WITH HERBS AND SPICES

Roasted grapes add intense flavour to a dish with their natural sweetness and juicy texture.

Makes 7–8 servings

Ingredients
3 cups red or black grapes (seedless)
4 sprigs rosemary
2 tbsp olive oil
3 red chillies, sliced
Salt to taste
½ tsp crushed black pepper

Method
Wash and dry the grapes.
Preheat the oven at 200°C.
Strip off the leaves from the rosemary stalks. Chop them roughly.
Toss the grapes in chopped rosemary, olive oil, sliced chillies, salt and pepper.
Spread out in a single layer in a baking tin or on a tray.
Roast at 200°C for around 30 minutes until the grapes are blistered on the outside.

How to use:
Add to a salad for an interesting element.
Top slices of sourdough baguette with goat's cheese and roasted grapes.
Mix into breakfast yoghurt.
Add to cooked pasta along with fresh herbs and parmesan cheese.
Serve along with a cheese platter and crackers.

TOMATO DATE CHILLI CHUTNEY

This chutney is inspired by flavours from Bengali cooking. The dates complement the tartness from the tomatoes beautifully.

Makes 1½ cups

Ingredients
8 medium-sized ripe tomatoes
¼ cup pitted dates
2 tbsp mustard oil
3–4 dried or fresh red chillies, sliced
½ tsp *kalonji* (onion seeds)
½ tsp fennel seeds
2 tsp grated ginger
2 tsp salt

Method

Roughly chop the tomatoes.
Soak the dates for 15 minutes in hot water. Drain and chop finely.
Heat the mustard oil in a heavy-bottomed pan.
Lower the flame, fry the chillies for a few seconds. Stir in the *kalonji* and fennel seeds. Once the aromas are released, fry the grated ginger for 30 seconds or so.
Add the chopped tomatoes and dates along with the salt and keep the flame on high.
Let this mixture come to a simmer. Reduce the flame, cover the pan and let it simmer for 30–40 minutes until the tomatoes are well cooked. Alternately, cook on a low flame in a pressure cooker with ¼ cup of water, for 10–15 minutes. Release the pressure, open the lid and simmer to let the remaining water evaporate. This cuts down the cooking time.
Allow the chutney to come to room temperature and save in an airtight container in the fridge.

How to use:
Use as a spread over toast.

Serve along with seeded crackers (page 198).

Thin this mixture with lime juice or oil and use as a salad dressing.

Serve along with *khichdi*.

Toss cooked chickpeas, finely chopped onions, green chillies and coriander along with this chutney.

Serve with parathas.

CORIANDER TURMERIC CHUTNEY

This super versatile green chutney that adds flavour to any meal is a must-stock in your refrigerator.

Makes 1 cup

Ingredients

4 cups coriander leaves
1 tsp turmeric powder or ½ inch fresh turmeric
3 green chillies
2 cloves garlic
2 tbsp roasted peanuts or fried gram
2 tbsp lime juice
1 tsp crushed jaggery
½ tsp fennel seeds
½ tsp salt

Method

Grind all the ingredients in the small jar of the food processor to a fine paste. Adjust salt depending on the heat in the chillies.

Keep in an airtight jar in the fridge.

How to use:

To make sandwiches.

Serve along with any breakfast/snacks.

Thin this chutney with extra virgin olive oil to use as a green salad dressing.

Combine with hung yoghurt to use as a dipping sauce or dressing.

MORINGA COCONUT CHUTNEY

This chutney is a nice way to make use of nutrition-dense *moringa* leaves. Try this recipe with any other DGLVs in season.

Makes 1 cup

Ingredients

2 tsp coconut oil, divided
2 cups *moringa* leaves
4 dried red chillies
1 tbsp *urad* dal
1 tbsp *chana* dal
1 tsp coriander seeds
1 piece tamarind flake
1 cup grated coconut
1 tsp salt

Method

In a pan, heat one teaspoon of coconut oil.

Finely chop the *moringa* leaves and sauté them in oil on a medium flame for 10–12 minutes until somewhat softened, adding a splash of water if it starts sticking to the pan. Remove and allow to cool.

Heat the remaining oil in the same pan. Fry chillies, dals, coriander seeds and tamarind until the dals turn golden brown. Remove this and allow it to cool.

In the same pan, toast grated coconut on a low flame until it turns fragrant and is slightly golden in colour.

Grind all the ingredients to a chutney along with the salt.

Variation: Increase the quantity of dals to three tablespoons each. Dry roast all the ingredients, including the leaves. Use desiccated coconut instead of fresh coconut and you have a *moringa* leaf *podi* that can be mixed with sesame or coconut oil and served with dosas and *idlis*.

How to use:

Mix with rice and ghee or have along with any south Indian breakfast dish.

SWEET AND SOUR TURMERIC PICKLE

Make batches of this pickle when fresh turmeric is in season. A bottle of this makes for a thoughtful edible gift for family and friends.

Makes 1 bottle

Ingredients

1 cup fresh turmeric root
¼ cup crushed jaggery
¼ cup apple cider vinegar
½ tsp black peppercorns, crushed
2 tsp salt

Method

Scrub and peel the turmeric root. Slice or cut into juliennes. Pack the chopped turmeric into a glass jar.

In a small pan, combine 1½ cups of water along with jaggery, vinegar, crushed black peppercorns and salt. Bring this to a simmer and allow the jaggery to dissolve. Pour over the packed turmeric in the glass jar. Shut the lid tightly and keep in the refrigerator for four to five days until it is ready to be eaten.

How to use:

Add a couple of tablespoons of this pickle to any salad.

Serve as an accompaniment to a meal.

Blend some of the pickled turmeric pieces along with chickpeas to make a turmeric hummus.

Finely chop the pickle and add to dal in the final stages.

SEEDED CRACKERS

Healthy home-made crackers are best for scooping up hummus and other dips, and make a healthy snack. Try a different combination of flours, seeds and flavours to come up with a new recipe each time.

Makes 6 servings

Ingredients

1 cup whole wheat flour
½ cup buckwheat flour
1 tbsp sesame seeds (mix of black and white)
1 tbsp flax seeds
1 tbsp poppy seeds
1 tsp fennel seeds
1 tsp salt
2 tbsp coconut oil
½ tsp instant yeast (or use sourdough starter)

Method

Combine all the dry ingredients in a bowl. Mix in coconut oil and yeast, combining well with fingertips.

Add water little by little to make a smooth but stiff dough.

Place the dough in an oiled bowl, covered with a lid or towel, for a minimum of one hour. Keeping it for three to four hours in the refrigerator gives it a better flavour.

Divide the dough into four portions. Roll out on a clean countertop into a very thin sheet.

Using a pizza cutter, cut the sheet into desired shapes.

Prepare a baking tray lined with a silicone mat or a baking paper.

Transfer the cut pieces to the tray, arranging in a single layer.

Bake in a preheated oven at 190°C for approximately eight minutes, keeping a close watch to prevent burning.

Serve with tomato chutney (page 192) or smoky beans (page 202).

MUHAMMARA WITH GREENS

Muhammara is a delicious hot pepper dip with origins in Aleppo, Syria. It is made in Turkey, Iraq, Lebanon and other Middle Eastern countries with small variations in ingredients. The addition of leafy greens makes this healthy dip all the more nutritious.

Makes 1½ cups

Ingredients

3 large red bell peppers
¼ cup walnut pieces
8–10 almonds, chopped
1 cup mixed green leafy vegetables
½ tsp chilli flakes
½ tsp smoked paprika (optional)
½ cup breadcrumbs (made from whole grain bread)
2 tbsp extra virgin olive oil
2 tbsp lime juice
1½ tsp salt
1–2 tsp extra virgin olive oil, for topping

Method

Apply a few drops of oil all over the bell peppers. Roast on an open flame until charred all over. Keep in a bowl and cover with a lid. After 10 minutes or so, the skins will loosen and can be easily peeled off. Roughly chop the flesh and discard the core, seeds and stem. Keep aside.

Toast the walnuts and almonds on the stovetop or in the microwave until aromatic and crisp.

Immerse greens in a pot of boiling water for two to three minutes. Remove the greens and plunge in a bowl of cold water. Squeeze dry.

In a food processor, combine the chopped bell pepper, toasted walnuts, and almonds, blanched greens, chilli flakes, paprika, breadcrumbs, extra virgin olive oil, lime juice and salt. Process to get a smooth paste.

Remove to a shallow bowl and top with extra olive oil.

How to use

Serve with seeded crackers (page 196), crudités or pita bread.

YOGHURT TAHINI DILL DRESSING

This dressing has all the goodness of sesame seeds and probiotics from the yoghurt. The nutty flavours from tahini and the herby fragrance from dill and fennel seeds give a unique taste to this dressing.

Makes 1 cup

Ingredients

1 cup hung yoghurt
1 tbsp tahini (sesame seed paste)
¼ cup dill leaves
¼ tsp fennel seed powder

2 tbsp extra virgin olive oil
½ tsp crushed black pepper
2 tbsp lime juice
½ tsp salt

Method

In a small mixer jar, blend together all ingredients except hung yoghurt until you get a fine puree.

Add the yoghurt to the blender and pulse a couple of times until everything is well combined, to get a thick, creamy dressing.

Keep refrigerated in a sealed glass jar and use within two to three days.

How to use:

Toss pasta in this dressing for a unique flavoured pasta dish. Top with toasted nuts and roasted grapes (page 193).

Toss oven-roasted spiced chickpeas in this dressing.

Serve with cucumber and carrot sticks.

Serve with a batch of savoury pancakes.

TURMERIC HONEY PEPPER DRESSING

Prepare this when fresh turmeric is in season. The slight bitterness in turmeric gets offset by the honey in the dressing. The active compounds in pepper facilitate better absorption of the antioxidants in turmeric, making this a winner superfood combination.

Makes 2 servings

Ingredients

1-inch piece of fresh turmeric
2 limes
1 tsp freshly crushed black pepper
2–3 tbsp honey
¼ cup extra virgin olive oil
½ tsp salt

Method

Scrub, peel and finely chop the fresh turmeric root.

Using a fine grater or zester, zest the lime peels.

Halve the limes and squeeze the lime juice, avoiding the seeds.

In a small mixer jar, combine chopped turmeric, black pepper, honey, lime zest, lime juice, extra virgin olive oil and salt. Use the pulse function to get a thick and creamy dressing.

On refrigerating, the oil will separate out. Whisk well and use.

How to use:

Use a couple of tablespoons of dressing over any salad. This dressing pairs well with hearty grain-based or root vegetable-based salads.

TAMARIND PEPPER SAUCE

The lip-smacking and pucker-inducing flavour of tamarind gives this sauce its addictive quality. It is inspired by the north Indian *meethi* chutney that goes into chaats, with pepper adding a bit of heat to complement the tanginess and sweetness.

Makes around 300 ml

Ingredients

½ cup tamarind
6–8 dates (seedless)
1 tsp fennel seeds
1 tsp cumin seeds
3 tbsp powdered jaggery
1½ tsp crushed black pepper
1 tsp turmeric powder
1 tsp salt

Method

Soak the tamarind in 1½ cups of hot water for 30 minutes. Squeeze out all the extract into the water. Strain this through a fine sieve, pressing out all the liquid.

Soak the dates in hot water for 30 minutes and grind to a coarse puree, using some of the soaking liquid.

Crush the fennel seeds to a coarse powder using a mortar and pestle.

Toast the cumin seeds in a small pan, until dark brown and aromatic. Crush this using a mortar and pestle to get a coarse powder.

In a pan, combine the tamarind extract, date puree, fennel and cumin powder, jaggery, black pepper, turmeric and salt. Bring this to a boil. Reduce the flame and simmer for 15 minutes or until the raw smell of tamarind is gone and the sauce has thickened. It should still be pourable from a spoon and not thickened into a paste.

Store this in an airtight container in the fridge for up to a month.

How to use:

This is your go-to sauce to make a variety of chaat-like snacks, but use healthier ingredients like boiled sweet potatoes, potatoes, mung sprouts, crispy puffed rice, etc.

This sauce complements a variety of root vegetables – boiled or oven-roasted.

Seasoned Brown Rice

Brown rice takes longer to cook than polished white rice. It is always a good idea to make a bigger batch of brown rice and store it in the fridge, to add healthy carbs to a quick meal. Seasoning the brown rice adds another layer of flavour to any dish that you might want to add it to, such as a salad or as a side for a beans curry.

Makes 6 servings

Ingredients

2 cups raw brown rice
1 tsp salt
2 tbsp coconut oil
2 tsp cumin seeds
2–3 green chillies, finely sliced
5–6 cloves of garlic, finely minced
1 tsp turmeric powder
3 tbsp lime juice

Method

Wash and soak the rice in plenty of water for one hour.

Drain the water. Place in a rice cooker or pressure cooker along with four cups of water and a teaspoon of salt. Pressure cook for 10 minutes (i.e., after full pressure or one whistle, keep on lowest heat setting for 10 minutes).

When the rice has been cooked, prepare the seasoning.

In a heavy-bottomed pan, heat the oil.

Stir in cumin seeds and once the seeds splutter, add the chillies and garlic and fry on a low flame. Do not let the garlic brown. Quickly stir in the turmeric and add the cooked brown rice. Stir gently to combine with seasoning. Turn off the flame, mix in the lime juice and reserve in airtight containers for use in several meals.

SPICED SMOKEY BEANS

A box of these beans is a ready go-to dose of protein that you can add to any meal. These also make excellent toppings for nachos or a side to a Mexican rice-based meal along with salsa.

Makes 2 cups

Ingredients

1 cup black-eyed peas
1 tsp salt
1 tbsp olive oil
5 cloves garlic, finely minced
1 tsp roasted cumin powder
1 tsp smoked paprika powder
 1 tsp chilli flakes
2 tsp dried oregano

Method

Soak the black-eyed peas in plenty of water for four to five hours.

Drain and place in a pressure cooker with three cups of water and a teaspoon of salt. Pressure cook for five minutes (i.e., after full pressure and one whistle, keep on lowest heat setting for five minutes).

Once cooled, drain through a colander and keep aside.

In a pan, heat the oil. On a low flame, sauté the garlic. Do not let it brown. Add the cooked beans, cumin powder, smoked paprika, chilli flakes and dried oregano. Stir to combine well.

Reserve in an airtight container in the fridge.

How to use:

Heat in the microwave before serving and top with fresh coriander and lime juice.

SUPERFOOD PORRIDGE MIX

Ragi is very rich in calcium. Soaking and sprouting improve the nutritional profile of this millet. Combining it with other protein-rich ingredients makes it a nutritious breakfast option.

Makes 2 cups

Ingredients

1 cup finger millet (ragi)
½ cup green mung
¼ cup soya beans
¼ cup fried gram (*dalia*)
¼ cup mix of walnuts, almonds, cashews

Method

Soak the ragi, soya beans and green mung for around nine hours. Drain well and spread out on cotton towels for another eight hours or so until dry.

Dry roast each of these ingredients in a hot pan or in the oven until all the moisture dries out. On toasting ragi, it will start popping and change to a darker shade. Both the mung and soya beans will also turn a few shades darker. Remove and cool all the ingredients.

Lightly toast the fried gram and nuts in the same pan, to dry out any moisture.

Either in a grain mill or in a mixer jar, grind all the ingredients to a fine powder.

The ragi alone can be powdered and sieved and used for porridge to make baby food.

You can prepare both sweet and savoury porridge using this mix.

Mix two tablespoons of powder with one cup of water, until dissolved. Bring this to a simmer until thickened and the flours are cooked. For a savoury version, add a pinch of salt and thinned yoghurt. For a sweet version, add organic jaggery and milk. Mix well and drink it hot or warm.

POMEGRANATE GINGER SHOTS

Makes 2 servings

Ingredients

1 cup shelled pomegranate arils
3-inch piece of ginger, grated
2 tsp honey

Method

In a blender, add the shelled pomegranate with half a cup of water. Pulse five to six times for a few seconds per pulse. Pass through a sieve into a bowl pressing down every bit of juice. Squeeze the grated ginger to release the juice into the bowl. Stir in the honey and pour into shot glasses. Drink immediately.

VG|V GREEN GODDESS JUICE

Makes 2 servings

Ingredients

3 cups mixed green leafy vegetables, chopped
2 *amlas*, quartered and seeds removed
½ green apple, cubed

Method

In a blender, add all the ingredients with ¼ cup water.
Pass through a sieve, pressing down every bit of juice. Pour into shot glasses and drink immediately. Sweeten with honey if required.

ICED PINEAPPLE GREEN TEA

Makes 2 servings

Ingredients

2 green tea bags or 2 tsp loose leaf tea
2 cups diced pineapple
1 lime
Ice cubes

Garnish:
Mint leaves
Pineapple wedges

Method

Brew tea bags or loose leaf tea in one cup of hot water for one minute. Don't use boiling water to brew green tea. Remove the tea bags (filter the tea leaves if using loose leaf) and add one cup of cold water to the brew. Chill this in the fridge.

Meanwhile, blend pineapple with half a cup of water. Pass through a sieve, pressing down every bit of juice. Add this prepared pineapple juice to the brewed and chilled green tea. Divide between two glasses. Add ice cubes and the juice of half a lime in each glass.

Use mint leaves and a pineapple wedge as garnish.

NUTMEGGY HOT COCOA

Makes 2 servings

Ingredients

2 tbsp cocoa powder
3 tsp raw cane sugar
Nutmeg for grating
2 cups milk (skimmed/whole/non-dairy milk)
Few drops vanilla extract

Method

In a small saucepan, whisk together cocoa, sugar and 2–3 pinches of freshly grated nutmeg. Add ¼ cup milk and whisk to get a smooth mixture. Add remaining milk and whisk well.

Turn on the flame and let this mixture come to a gentle simmer. Do not over boil. Remove from heat and add the vanilla with a small pinch of grated nutmeg.

Divide between two cups and serve hot.

Ground cinnamon, ground ginger or chai masala are good substitutes for nutmeg in this recipe.

WHEATGRASS BLACK PEPPER HONEY SHOTS

Makes 2 servings

Ingredients

1 cup chopped wheatgrass
¼ tsp freshly ground black pepper
2 tsp honey

2 tsp lime juice

Method

Add chopped wheatgrass and 60 millilitres of water to a mixer jar. Blend well. Pass through a sieve, pressing down every bit of juice. Mix in black pepper, honey and lime juice. Divide between two small glasses. Drink immediately.

TAMARIND MINT APPETIZER DRINK

Makes 6 servings

Ingredients

3 tbsp tamarind (packed)
1 cup mint leaves (packed)
4 slices fresh ginger
1 tsp cumin seeds
1 tsp fennel seeds

4 tbsp jaggery
1 tbsp black salt
Juice of 1 lime

Method

In a bowl, add a cup of hot water over the tamarind and allow it to soften for 15 minutes. Squeeze well, using your fingers to get the tamarind extract. Discard the tamarind pieces.

In a mixer jar, blend the mint, ginger, cumin seeds, fennel seeds and jaggery, using ¼ cup water.

Mix this green paste with the tamarind extract. Add a litre of water, the black salt and lime juice to this mix. Allow this to sit in the fridge for two hours. Pass the mixture through a sieve and it is ready to serve. Serve as a digestive drink ahead of a meal or as a coolant on summer days.

TURMERIC GINGER HOLY BASIL HEALING TEA

Makes 2 servings

Ingredients

4–5 slices of fresh turmeric
4–5 slices of fresh ginger
Handful holy basil or *tulsi* leaves
2 tsp honey
½ lime

Method

In a saucepan, bring two cups of water to a boil.

Using a mortar and pestle, crush the turmeric and ginger. Add the holy basil and crush the leaves.

Transfer this to the boiling water. Allow it to simmer for two to three minutes. Turn off the flame. Cover the pan, allowing the infusion to steep for ten minutes. Pass the tea through a filter into two cups. Mix in the honey and juice of a quarter of lime in each cup. Serve warm any time of the day or when a bad throat needs a healing touch. It is also suitable for kids.

BORICHA – KOREAN ROASTED BARLEY TEA

Boricha is a Korean grain-based tea that can be had hot or cold. It is 100 per cent caffeine-free, making it a good choice for a late evening beverage if caffeinated drinks prevent you from getting a good night's sleep. In Korea, pre-roasted barley is available for the purpose of making tea. It is even available as tea bags.

Makes 6 servings

Ingredients

2 tbsp barley seeds

Method

In a pan, dry roast the barley seeds on a low flame for 15 minutes or so until deeply aromatic.

In a saucepan bring one litre of water to a boil. Add the roasted barley seeds to the boiling water and simmer for five minutes. Pass through a sieve and either drink the tea warm or refrigerate in a jug and drink it cold.

BREAKFAST

BANANA PINEAPPLE GREEN TEA SMOOTHIE

This green smoothie has a hearty serving of antioxidants from green tea and *moringa*. Bananas and pineapple add natural sweetness and extra fibre.

Makes 1 serving

Ingredient

1 tea bag green tea (or 1 tsp loose leaf green tea)*

2 frozen bananas (small)

2 slices pineapple

1 tsp *moringa* powder
8–10 spinach leaves

Method

Brew green tea with ¾ cup of water. Do not use boiling hot water to brew the tea.

In a blender, add the frozen bananas, pineapple, *moringa* powder, spinach leaves, and brewed green tea. Blend until it is smooth, and no chunks remain.

Pour into a glass and drink immediately.

*use 1 tsp matcha powder instead, if available.

CHOCOLATE AVOCADO CINNAMON SMOOTHIE

This smoothie is an almost dessert for breakfast. It's a good way to use up a ripe avocado when not in the mood for guacamole and chips.

Makes 1 serving

Ingredients

½ medium avocado (ripe*)
1 banana
½ tsp ground cinnamon
1 tsp cacao powder
¼ cup yoghurt
1 tbsp honey
½ cup water

Method

For best results, keep the avocado and banana in the freezer beforehand. To the mixer jar or blender, add the frozen avocado, banana, cinnamon, cacao powder, yoghurt, honey and ½ cup water. Blend until no chunks remain.

Serve immediately in a tall glass.

*read the note on how to get perfectly ripe avocado on page 34

POPPED AMARANTH CHOCOLATE GRANOLA

Gourmet food stores stock up on a variety of (expensive) artisanal granolas. Here is one such delicious granola that you can make at home for a fraction of the cost.

Makes 10–12 servings

Ingredients

1 cup mixed dried fruit (dates, raisins, apricots, figs)
1 cup mixed nuts
1 cup amaranth (the whole grain)
½ cup dried coconut flakes
1 cup rolled oats
¼ cup date puree
2 tbsp coconut oil
½ cup chopped dark chocolate (or chocolate chips)

Method

Chop the dried fruit and nuts into bite-sized pieces.

In a preheated heavy-bottomed pan, place ¼ cup amaranth at a time. Cover with a lid and allow to pop completely. Remove this to a dish and similarly, pop the remaining amaranth in batches.

Toss the popped amaranth along with the nuts, dried fruits, and coconut oil and spread out in a single layer on a baking tray.

Bake in a preheated oven at 180°C for 30 minutes.

Place chopped chocolate in a dry microwave-safe bowl and heat in bursts of 30 seconds at one time and give it a stir. Repeat until it is fully melted.

Pour the melted chocolate over the toasted granola, mixing it into some clusters. Allow to cool completely so that the chocolate coats some bits of granola and some are left as it is.

Once it is at room temperature, save in an airtight container.

Serve with milk or yoghurt.

PINEAPPLE POMEGRANATE YOGHURT BOWLS

Yoghurt bowls are a rage in healthy brunch menus around the world. Think of plain yoghurt as a canvas for all your favourite superfood ingredients. Feel free to play around using whichever fruits are in season.

Makes 2 servings

Ingredients

4 slices pineapples
2 cups yoghurt
4 tbsp pomegranate arils
4 tbsp mung sprouts
2 tbsp mixed TNST (page 192)
1 tbsp hemp hearts

Method

Chop the pineapple into centimetre-sized pieces.
Whisk yoghurt until free of lumps and divide it between two bowls. Mix in pomegranate, pineapple and mung sprouts.
Top with TNST and hemp hearts.
Serve chilled.

OATS AMLA UPMA

Oats *upma* is way quicker to make than the traditional *rava upma*, especially if using instant oats. For those who like a hot savoury breakfast, this one will hit the spot with a megadose of antioxidants from *amla*.

Makes 2 large servings

Ingredients

1 cup instant oats
1 tbsp coconut oil
1 tsp grated ginger

2 green chillies
1 sprig curry leaves
½ tsp mustard seeds
1 tomato, chopped
2 *amlas* in brine (page 188), chopped
¾ tsp salt
2 tbsp yoghurt
2 tbsp grated coconut

Method

In a pan, toast the oats for one to two minutes until aromatic. Remove into a dish.

Heat the oil in the pan. Fry the ginger, green chillies, curry leaves and mustard seeds.

Once the mustard seeds pop, add the chopped tomato and *amla*. Add salt and stir until the tomatoes are nearly cooked.

Add two cups of water. Stir in the yoghurt.

Once this comes to a boil, reduce the flame and add oats, stirring constantly. Cover and cook for three to four minutes.

Let it sit covered for 10 minutes or until all the water is absorbed.

Serve hot with a garnish of grated coconut.

BUCKWHEAT FLOUR TOMATO DOSAS

With a bit of prep work the previous night, this is a fairly low effort breakfast to make. High in fibre buckwheat flour adds to the satiety quotient of these dosas.

Makes 6–8 dosas

Ingredients

1 cup buckwheat flour
½ cup rice flour
2 tbsp sour yoghurt
3 tomatoes (medium-sized)
1 tsp salt
Oil to make dosas (cold-pressed gingelly oil)

Method

Mix the flours in a bowl. To this, add yoghurt and 1½ cups of water. Whisk well and allow to soak overnight.

Blend the tomatoes to get a puree and add it to the fermented batter. Mix in salt.

Lightly grease a dosa *tawa* with oil. A cast-iron *tawa* is recommended although new cooks may find it easier to use a non-stick *tawa*.

Pour 1–2 ladles of the batter in the centre of the tawa and spread outward in circles. Do not make the dosa too thin.

Pour a teaspoon of oil around the dosa and cook for one minute or so on medium flame. Flip over and cook the other side for another minute until somewhat crisp.

Serve hot with any chutney of choice. Try it with the *moringa* coconut chutney (page 196).

MILLET SURNOLI

Surnoli is an addictive sweet-savoury fermented pancake from Mangaluru in Karnataka. This recipe harnesses the goodness of lesser processed ingredients like red rice and red rice *poha*. Millets add to its nutrient quotient.

Ingredients

½ cup red rice
½ cup foxtail millet or little millet
2 tsp fenugreek seeds
½ cup red rice *poha*
1 tsp turmeric
1 cup yoghurt
¼ cup grated coconut
1 tsp salt
3–4 tbsp jaggery
Ghee to cook

Method

Soak the red rice, millet and fenugreek seeds for four hours.

Soak the *poha* along with the turmeric in yoghurt for one hour.

Drain the soaked rice, millet and fenugreek, and grind to a fine paste, using very little water as required. To this, add the soaked *poha*-yoghurt mixture and coconut. Grind to a fine paste.

Remove this to a bowl. Cover with a lid and allow the mix to ferment overnight.

Add salt and jaggery to the batter, mix well.

Pour ⅓ cup batter on a flat *tawa*, allowing it to spread out naturally. You will see lots of air bubbles on the surface and around the circumference of the *surnoli*. Use a little ghee around the sides to aid cooking. Flip the *surnoli* and cook for another one minute or so before removing it to a plate.

Eat as it is or serve with chutney.

SALADS

BLACK-EYED PEAS, CHARGRILLED CORN AND ROCKET SALAD

The charred corn, the punch from the rocket leaves and the puckering freshness from the tamarind pepper sauce add a whole lot of flavour and fun to this hearty salad. Make your own variation of this salad by substituting the beans and greens using whichever varieties you have on hand.

Makes 2–3 servings

Ingredients

½ cup dried black-eyed peas
1 small onion
2 tbsp apple cider vinegar
Pinch of salt
1 piece corn on the cob
2 handfuls of rocket/arugula
1 small European cucumber

Dressing:
1 tbsp apple cider vinegar
1 tbsp apple chutney (or use any fruit preserve)
2 tbsp extra virgin olive oil
Salt

Garnish:
Pinch of red chilli flakes

Method

Soak the black-eyed peas in a bowl of water for four hours. Drain and cook with fresh water, either on a stovetop or in the pressure cooker until just cooked and retaining its shape. The cooking time will depend on the size of the beans, but it will take roughly 20 minutes using the boiling method on the stovetop or five minutes at full pressure in a pressure cooker. Drain the cooked beans and keep aside. If you have cooked beans or canned beans, then this step can be skipped.

Peel and slice the onion. Crush the slices with your fingertips to separate the onion into segments. Place this in a bowl with the apple cider vinegar and a pinch of salt. Cover and keep aside for 15 minutes. This method of quick pickling takes the bite out of the onions and makes it taste better in salads.

Roast the corn on an open flame until black spots appear all around. Using a sharp knife, shuck the corn kernels into a bowl.

Wash the rocket leaves in two to three changes of water until totally free of any grit. Drain well on cotton towels or in a salad spinner.

Slice the cucumber into half-moons. If using the larger variety, peel and scoop out the seeds before slicing.

In a bowl, combine the cooked black-eyed peas, corn, rocket and cucumber. Squeeze the onion segments to get rid of all the excess vinegar and add it to the salad.

Mix all the ingredients for the dressing in a small bowl until well combined.

Toss the salad in the dressing and garnish with chilli flakes.

Serve immediately.

Sweet Potato Chaat

This chaat has enough health-boosting nutrients to be able to call itself a salad. Prepare the chutneys as a part of your weekly meal prep so that this chaat is ready in a matter of minutes.

Makes 2 servings

Ingredients

1 medium sweet potato
1–2 tsp cold-pressed sunflower oil
1 medium onion
1 large tomato
1 green chilli
2 tbsp chopped coriander leaves
2–3 tbsp coriander turmeric chutney (page 193)
2–3 tbsp tomato date chilli chutney (page 192)

Garnish:
Chaat masala
Red chilli powder
Coriander leaves
2–3 tbsp crushed roasted peanuts
½ lime

Method

Scrub and wash the sweet potatoes. Cut into thin slices (<½ cm). Toss in 1–2 tsp cold-pressed sunflower oil. Lay out on a greased baking tray and bake at 180°C for seven to eight minutes until golden brown spots appear on the slices. The slices should somewhat crisp up. Keep an eye on the oven so that the sweet potato slices don't burn. Alternatively, lay out the slices on a lightly greased flat pan (*tawa*) and cook each side for three to four minutes.

While the sweet potato slices are cooking, prepare the topping.

Chop the onion and tomato very finely. Combine with sliced green chilli and chopped coriander in a bowl.

On a platter, lay out the sweet potato slices in a single layer.

Smear some coriander turmeric chutney over the sweet potato. Place a teaspoon of the onion-tomato mix on each slice. Top with ½ tsp of tomato date chutney.

Garnish with a sprinkle of chaat masala, red chilli powder and finely chopped coriander. Top all the slices with a bit of crushed roasted peanuts. Squeeze lime all around the platter and serve immediately.

AMARANTH SALAD

This salad makes use of all parts of green amaranth. For this salad, choose amaranth leaves with a few flowers. These are bright red tassels that hold the amaranth seeds.

This makes for a simple side dish to a dal-rice meal. Play around with the flavours by using a combination of mustard oil and *kalonji* seeds or coconut oil and cumin seeds.

Makes 2 servings

Ingredients

1 bunch amaranth leaves (red or green)
2 tbsp olive oil
1 tsp finely chopped garlic
1 medium-sized carrot
Juice of 1 lime
Pinch of salt
1 tbsp white sesame seeds

Method

Pick out the tender small leaves from the bunch to use raw in the salad. Pluck the larger and more mature leaves to be sautéed. Wash and drain both leaves separately.

In a pan, heat one teaspoon of oil. Fry chopped garlic for a few seconds and add the larger leaves. Sauté on a high flame for one to two minutes until it is wilted. Keep aside and allow to cool completely.

Peel and coarsely grate the carrot.

Take two to three bunches of amaranth flowers and chop it finely.

In a bowl, toss the smaller leaves, grated carrot and chopped flowers in one teaspoon of olive oil and two teaspoons of lime juice along with a pinch of salt.

In a bowl or platter, combine the sautéed amaranth leaves along with the carrot and amaranth mix. Top with the remaining oil, lime juice and sesame seeds.

ROASTED PUMPKIN AND MASSAGED DGLV SALAD

The contrasting colours of the pumpkin and the greens makes this a visually appealing salad, apart from being highly nutritious. Use any of the dark green local leafy greens in season. Instead of oven roasting the pumpkin, it can be cut into cubes and can also be slow-roasted on a cast-iron pan.

 Makes 2 servings

Ingredients

2 cups pumpkin cubes 1-inch size (dark orange variety)
1 tbsp coconut oil
½ tsp salt
½ tsp roasted cumin powder
2 cups mix of DGLVs
1 tbsp lime juice
Pinch of salt
¼ cup whole *masoor* dal, soaked for 2 hours

Dressing:
½ tbsp olive oil
1 tsp wholegrain mustard
1 tbsp lime juice
Pinch of salt

Garnish:
Dried coconut slices
TNST (page 190)

Method

Preheat the oven at 190°C.

Toss the pumpkin cubes in a teaspoon of coconut oil, roasted cumin powder and ¼ tsp salt. Arrange it on a baking tray or tin and roast for 40 minutes until golden brown spots appear on the outside and the pumpkin is cooked through. Remove and cool to room temperature.

Prepare the DGLVs by using only the leaves and tender stems and discarding the hard stalks. Place the washed and dried greens in a bowl. Top with two teaspoons of coconut oil, lime juice and a pinch of salt. Massage this well into the leaves with a firm hand. Cover and keep aside for 30 minutes. You could also keep a heavy ceramic bowl as a weight over the greens, to soften them a bit.

Drain the pre-soaked *masoor* and cook with fresh water and a pinch of salt for 20 minutes or so on a stovetop, until cooked but retaining its shape. Drain and cool to room temperature.

Toast the dried coconut slices either in a microwave or in a heavy-bottomed pan until golden brown and aromatic.

To assemble the salad, make a bed of the massaged greens. Scatter the roasted pumpkin cubes over the bed of greens. Spoon the cooked *masoor* around the platter.

In a small bowl, whisk the dressing ingredients until creamy and thick.

Spoon the dressing all around the salad.

Top with toasted coconut slices and TNST.

Serve immediately.

Add ½ cup of seasoned brown rice (page 201) to this salad to make it a complete meal.

RED GRAPES AND MUNG SPROUTS SALAD

Mung sprouts and paneer are commonly found ingredients in an Indian kitchen. Combining it with seasonal red and green grapes makes it an interesting salad full of colours and natural sweetness.

Makes 2 servings

Ingredients

1 cup red or black seedless grapes
¼ cup green grapes
100 grams paneer or tofu
½ red bell pepper
1 cup mung sprouts
Handful of microgreens

Dressing:
2 tbsp extra virgin olive oil
2 tsp balsamic vinegar or malt vinegar
¼ tsp very finely grated ginger
¼ tsp salt
½ tsp black pepper

Method

Wash and dry the grapes. Cut the black grapes into halves. Leave the green grapes intact.

De-seed and dice the bell pepper.

Dice the paneer in a similar size.

In a bowl, mix together the grapes, mung sprouts and bell pepper.

Separately, mix all the dressing ingredients in a small bowl until thick and creamy. Combine the dressing with the ingredients in the bowl. Add the paneer cubes towards the end and mix gently.

Serve chilled.

BROCCOLI, APPLE AND WALNUT SALAD

These three ingredients make a classic trio for a simple salad. Using a mix of green and red apples adds to the colour in the salad bowl. Toasted walnuts add to the crunch and flavour of the salad.

Makes 2–4 servings

Ingredients

1 green apple
1 red apple
2 cups steamed broccoli
10–12 walnut halves

Dressing:
1 tbsp wholegrain mustard
1 tbsp honey
2 tsp apple cider vinegar
1½ tbsp extra virgin olive oil
¼ tsp salt
½ tsp ground black pepper

Method

Chop the red and green apple into bite-sized pieces.
In a large bowl, combine the broccoli and apples.
In a small bowl, whisk the dressing ingredients until thick and creamy.
Pour the dressing over the broccoli and apples and toss well.
Toast the walnut halves in a pan over a low flame for three to four minutes until crisp. Garnish the salad with toasted walnuts.

AVOCADO POMELO SALAD

There are a lot of ways to eat a perfectly ripe avocado and this colourful salad is one of them. Use orange or sweet lime segments if pomelo is not in season.

Makes 2 servings

Ingredients

½ medium-sized avocado (ripe)
1 large carrot
1 medium cucumber
1 green capsicum
½ cup pomelo segments
1 small red chilli, sliced
¼ cup pomegranate arils
1 tbsp lime juice
2 tsp extra virgin olive oil
¼ tsp salt
2 tbsp TNST (page 190)

Garnish:
1 tbsp hemp hearts
2 tsp hemp seed oil

Method

Scoop out the avocado flesh from the skin. Cut into two-centimetre-sized cubes.
Wash and scrub the carrot and cucumber. Peel them into thin strips using a vegetable peeler.
Slice the green capsicum into thin matchsticks, discarding the core and seeds.
In a bowl, gently combine the avocado, carrot, cucumber, capsicum, pomelo, chilli, pomegranate and lime juice.

Add the extra virgin olive oil and salt and toss very gently with your fingertips so as not to crush the pomelo or smash the ripe avocado cubes. Sprinkle the TNST and give it a final mix.

Divide between two bowls. Top each serving with a sprinkling of hemp hearts and a touch of hemp seed oil.

ROASTED CAULIFLOWER WITH HUNG YOGHURT DIP

Turn cauliflower into an interesting appetizer/salad with a minimal list of ingredients. The yoghurt needs to be strained for a minimum of three to four hours, so it helps to be prepped in advance.

Makes 2 servings

Ingredients

1 medium cauliflower
2 tsp salt
½ tsp turmeric
1 tbsp coconut oil
½ tsp salt

Yoghurt dip:
2 cups yoghurt
1 garlic clove
½ lime
1 small bunch of dill leaves
¼ tsp salt
1 tsp black sesame seeds

Method

Prepare the hung yoghurt well in advance. Place a sieve over a bowl. Line the sieve with a double layer of muslin cloth. Empty the yoghurt over this. Bring together and knot the corners of the cloth. Place this set-up in the refrigerator for three to four hours. The whey will get collected in the bowl below and the thick yoghurt in the sieve is to be used for the recipe. To go through this process in a shorter while, use Greek yoghurt, which could be used as-is or after just 30 minutes to an hour of resting in the muslin cloth.

Break the cauliflower into florets. Immerse in a bowl of water salted with two teaspoons of salt for around 15–20 minutes. Shake off each floret and wash in fresh water. Dry the florets thoroughly using a cotton towel.

Preheat the oven at 190°C.

Toss the cauliflower florets in oil, turmeric powder and salt.

Spread it on a baking tray and bake at 190°C for 25–30 minutes until charred spots appear on the surface of the florets.

While the cauliflower is roasting, transfer the hung yoghurt to a bowl. Using a fork, whisk until smooth. Grate the garlic clove into the yoghurt. Grate the lime zest from the skin of the lime over the yoghurt and squeeze juice from half the lime.

Chop dill leaves finely and add to the yoghurt. Season with salt and whisk well to combine. Transfer to a bowl and top with black sesame seeds.

Prepare the same recipe using broccoli or a mix of veggies like bell peppers, zucchini or radish roasted in the oven. This makes for a healthy appetizer or a light lunch.

POMELO AND BETEL LEAF SALAD

The sharp spicy flavours of the betel leaf offset the mild sweetness of the pomelo segments. This salad makes a healthy and vibrant appetizer for a party. Use lettuce leaves to make individual parcels in case betel leaves are not available.

Makes 2–3 servings

Ingredients

1 small cucumber
2 fresh red chillies
2–3 tbsp coriander leaves
1 small green mango, shredded

Handful of Thai basil leaves
2 tbsp grated coconut
1 cup pomelo segments
8 medium-sized betel leaves
2 tbsp roasted and skinned peanuts

Dressing:
2 tbsp soy sauce
1 tsp white vinegar
1 tbsp honey
1 tsp chilli sauce or 1 red chilli, minced

Method

Wash and peel the cucumber into strips.

Finely slice the red chillies.

Finely chop the coriander leaves.

In a bowl, toss together cucumber, green mango, Thai basil, red chillies, coriander and coconut. Add the pomelo towards the end and give it a final gentle toss.

On a platter, lay out the betel leaves.

Pile the salad over each leaf. Top with a bit of dressing and crushed roasted peanuts.

To eat, scrunch up the betel leaf into a parcel and eat the salad as one mouthful.

Alternatively, pile up the betel leaves and slice them thinly. Toss the sliced leaves along with the rest of the ingredients and serve the salad in a bowl.

MAINS

BLACK-EYED PEAS IN GINGER-GARLIC SAUCE

This makes for a hearty, fibre-rich main course dish served along with rice or noodles. Dried beans need a few hours of soaking for this dish. Saving cooked beans in the refrigerator makes this a very quick dish to prepare.

Ingredients

½ cup dried black-eyed peas
½ tsp salt
1-inch piece ginger
8 cloves garlic
3 green chillies
1 small green capsicum
1 small onion
1 tbsp groundnut oil
2 tsp corn flour
½ cup water
2 tbsp dark soy sauce
2 tbsp white vinegar
1 tbsp honey
1 sprig spring onion greens

Method

Soak the black-eyed peas for four to five hours. Drain and add the black-eyed peas to a pressure cooker along with 1½ cups of water and a half teaspoon of salt.

Pressure cook for five minutes (i.e., after full pressure and one whistle, keep on lowest heat setting for five minutes) or 15–20 minutes of boiling on a stovetop. Cooking time depends upon the size of the beans. Drain the beans and keep aside.

Peel and chop the ginger and garlic very finely. Slice the green chillies. Peel and chop the onion and capsicum into centimetre-sized pieces.

Heat the groundnut oil in a pan. Stir the ginger and garlic for a few seconds, making sure not to brown the garlic. Fry the chillies, onion and green capsicum over a high flame for a minute, allowing the vegetables to remain crunchy.

Make a slurry of corn flour in half a cup of water.

Add the soy sauce, vinegar, honey and the corn flour slurry to the pan. Allow this to come to a simmer. Once the sauce thickens, add the cooked black-eyed peas and bring to a boil, then let it simmer for three to four minutes.

Garnish with spring onion greens. Serve with steamed rice.

MILLETS IN TOMATO SAUCE PARCELS

This recipe is an interesting way of presenting an ancient grain. The process of cooking in leaf parcels is not new in Indian cuisine. The leaves seal the aromas inside the parcels while imparting their own subtle flavour to the food.

Makes 6 parcels

Ingredients

For millets:
1 cup foxtail millet
1 tsp salt
1 tsp olive oil

For sauce:
6 large ripe tomatoes
6 cloves garlic
1 small onion
1 tbsp olive oil
1 tbsp mixed dried herbs
½ tsp red chilli flakes
1 ½ tsp salt
1 tsp raw sugar
Handful of fresh herbs (choose from rosemary, basil, parsley)

For parcels:
6 squares banana leaves
Toothpicks or twine to secure
2 tsp oil

Method

Wash, rinse and drain the millets. Soak them in a bowl of water for two to three hours. Drain and place in a pan with 1½ cups of water, salt and olive oil. Cover the pan and cook for 5–7 minutes over a low flame. Fluff up the cooked grains with a fork and remove to a bowl.

To prepare the sauce, bring a pot of water to boil. Lightly score an 'X' mark near the stem end of the tomatoes and drop them into boiling water. Simmer the tomatoes for four to five minutes, or until the skins start to come off. Remove the tomatoes using a slotted spoon and immerse in a bowl of cold water for five minutes. Peel off the skins and finely chop the tomatoes.

Finely chop the garlic cloves and onion.

Heat olive oil in a pan. Fry the chopped garlic for a few seconds, taking care not to let it brown.

Add the onion and sauté for 4–5 minutes.

Transfer the chopped blanched tomatoes, dried herbs, chilli flakes, salt and sugar to the pan. Combine well and simmer for around ten minutes until the sauce thickens up and comes together.

Chop fresh herbs finely and stir in half the quantity into the sauce.

To prepare the parcels, scald the leaves for a few seconds on each side over a hot pan. This makes them pliable and ensures that they don't tear upon folding.

Place ¼ cup cooked millet in the centre of the leaf square. Top with 3–4 tablespoons of sauce. Sprinkle a bit of the fresh herbs over this with a few drops of olive oil.

Fold the leaf to make a parcel and secure with twine or toothpick.

Lightly grease a hot pan. Place the leaf parcels two to three at a time. Allow each side to cook for 2–3 minutes. Keep warm until ready to serve. Serve the entire parcel as is. Untie/remove the toothpick just before eating.

SWEET POTATO IN TAMARIND SAUCE (KUZHAMBU)

This is a traditional Tamil recipe that is had with rice or any other cooked grains. It gets ready rather quickly as compared to *sambar* as there is no need to cook dal for this recipe. Use cubes of yellow pumpkin instead of sweet potato or broad beans or a combination of all three vegetables.

Makes 2–3 servings

Ingredients

2 tablespoons tamarind (medium lime-sized ball)
1 cup boiling hot water
2 medium-sized sweet potatoes
2 tbsp cold-pressed gingelly oil
¼ tsp fenugreek seeds
½ tsp mustard seeds
1 tbsp *tur* dal (raw)
2 sprigs curry leaves
2–3 dried red chillies
1 pinch asafoetida
½ tsp turmeric powder
2 tbsp *sambar* powder
1 tsp salt
2 tsp rice flour

Method

Place the tamarind in a bowl. Pour hot water to cover and keep aside for 15 minutes. Squeeze to extract all the pulp from the tamarind into the hot water. Discard the tamarind pieces and reserve the extract.

Scrub the sweet potatoes and wash well. Do not peel. Chop into centimetre-thick slices.

Heat oil in a pan. Fry the fenugreek seeds, mustard seeds, *tur* dal, curry leaves and red chillies. Wait until the *tur* dal turns golden brown and the mustard seeds splutter. Stir in the asafoetida and sweet potato slices. Fry for one to two minutes.

Add the tamarind extract, turmeric, *sambar* powder and salt. Add a cup of hot water to the pan. Cover and boil for five to six minutes or until the sweet potato slices are cooked.

Make a slurry of rice flour in ¼ cup water and add it to the simmering *kuzhambu*. Boil this for two to three minutes.

The end result will be a pourable sauce-like consistency with cooked sweet potatoes.

Serve with steamed rice or millets.

BROCCOLI PAKODIS IN KADHI

This is a superfood take on the *kadhi pakodi*, in which the onion pakoras are replaced by pan-fried broccoli *pakodis*. If you do not mind the deep frying, then, by all means, dip florets of broccoli in a chickpea-flour batter and use that in the prepared *kadhi*.

Makes 4 servings

Ingredients

For the *pakodis*:
1 cup coarsely grated broccoli
1 cup besan (gram flour)
3 tbsp yoghurt
¼ tsp turmeric
Pinch of asafoetida
2 tsp ginger-green chilli paste
1 tsp salt

½ tsp baking soda
2 tsp oil
Oil for cooking

For the *kadhi*:
1½ cups yoghurt
2 tbsp gram flour
1 tsp ginger-green chilli paste
1 tsp salt
¼ tsp turmeric
2 tsp oil
2 dried red chillies
1 tsp cumin seeds
1 sprig curry leaves
Pinch of asafoetida

Method

In a bowl, mix together all ingredients for the *pakodis*, except the oil for cooking. Add a little water if required, to get a thick batter (like an *idli* batter consistency).

Use a *paniyaram* pan for making the *pakodis*. Grease the cavities with a little oil. When hot, put two spoonfuls of batter in each cavity (or until three-fourth filled). Add a few drops of oil around each *pakodi*. Cook on a low flame for three to four minutes until golden and crisp on one side. Flip over and cook the other side similarly. Make three batches or so until all the batter is used up.

To prepare the *kadhi*, whisk in gram flour, ginger-green chilli paste, salt and turmeric into the yoghurt to get a lump-free mix. Add two cups of water to this and whisk to combine.

Bring this to a simmer on low heat with constant stirring. Leaving it on the flame without stirring may cause the yoghurt to split.

Meanwhile, heat the oil for tempering. Fry dried red chillies, cumin seeds and curry leaves. Once the seeds splutter, quickly stir in the asafoetida and transfer the tempering over the *kadhi*.

Just before serving, add the *pakodis* to the *kadhi* and serve hot with steamed rice.

Note: If the yoghurt is too sour, add a couple of teaspoons of raw sugar to the *kadhi* mixture to balance out the sourness.

SPROUTED MUNG AND PINEAPPLE CURRY

An unusual combination of ingredients comes together in this coconut milk-based curry that can be had with rice or noodles.

Makes 3 servings

Ingredients

For the spice paste:
8–10 Thai basil leaves
2 fresh red chillies
4 cloves garlic
1-inch piece ginger or galangal

3-inch lemongrass stalk
6–7 coriander stems
1 tbsp coriander seeds
3–4 lime leaves or zest from 1 lime

For the curry:
1 tbsp coconut oil
1 cup mung sprouts
2 cups diced pineapple
½ cup diced green zucchini
8–10 Thai basil leaves
200 ml coconut milk
½ tsp salt

Method

Grind all the ingredients for the spice paste in a small mixer jar until you get a smooth paste. Add 2–3 tablespoons of water while grinding, if required.

Heat the oil in a pan. Fry the prepared spice paste over low heat for two to three minutes. Add the mung sprouts and pineapple. Sauté over medium flame for two to three minutes. Add ½ cup hot water, cover the pan and cook for five to seven minutes until the sprouts and pineapple are somewhat tender. Add the diced zucchini and allow to cook on high flame for two minutes.

Mix in coconut milk and salt, along with torn basil leaves. Bring to a simmer and remove from flame. Serve with steamed rice.

Note: Use seasonal vegetables like diced eggplant, bell peppers, pumpkin, etc., in this curry.

SWEET POTATO BUCKWHEAT FLATBREADS

Serve these flatbreads with a curry on the side for the main course or use it to scoop dips, or use it as a pizza base.

Makes 3–4 portions

Ingredients

1½ tsp instant yeast
1 tsp sugar
½ cup warm milk
1 cup buckwheat flour
½ cup whole wheat flour
2 tsp crushed dried oregano
½ tsp crushed red chilli flakes
1 tsp salt
½ cup mashed sweet potato
2 tbsp finely chopped garlic
1 tbsp oil + more to cook if required

Method

While instant yeast does not need activation, it is good to check if it is in an active state before mixing it with all the ingredients. In a cup, mix the instant yeast with sugar and warm milk. Stir well and keep covered for 10 minutes until the mixture is frothy.

In a big bowl, combine the flours, oregano, chilli flakes and salt. Mix the mashed sweet potato into the dry mixture. Make a well in the centre and add the yeast mixture, slowly working it into the ingredients to make a soft dough.

Grease a bowl with oil. Place the dough in the bowl and keep it covered for one to two hours until doubled in volume. This depends on the room temperature. On a hot day, 45 minutes may be enough.

Divide the dough into four balls. Cover this with a cotton towel and allow the dough to rest for another 15–20 minutes.

Using a bit of whole wheat flour to dust, and a rolling pin with a board, roll out each ball into thin oval-shaped flatbreads, similar to naan.

Sprinkle ½ tbsp of chopped garlic over each flatbread and gently roll over with the rolling pin so that the garlic sticks.

To cook, either bake in a preheated 190°C oven for 10 minutes, flipping over midway, or cook on a flat pan on the stovetop, for two to three minutes over medium heat on each side. Brush with oil on both sides while cooking.

Note: Mashed potato can be used for the same recipe. Use a mix of Indian herbs and spices such as chopped coriander, grated ginger, sliced green chillies, coriander powder and *amchur* or *anardaana* powder for an Indian-flavoured flatbread that can be served with green chutney.

DGLV STEW WITH BLACK-EYED PEAS

Even if yours is a smaller family, prepare the entire quantity. Leftovers can be refrigerated and used over the next two days. This hearty nutrient-rich stew is a perfect meal to serve on a winter evening.

Makes a big pot with 6–8 servings

Ingredients

1 cup black-eyed peas (dry), soaked overnight

2 tsp salt, divided
3 tbsp olive oil
3 bay leaves
10 cloves garlic
2 onions, finely chopped
1 large carrot, finely chopped
8 cups mixed DGLVs (packed)*
4 cups tomato puree
2 tsp cumin powder
1 tsp turmeric powder
1 tsp red chilli powder or paprika

Method

Drain and rinse the soaked beans. Place in a pressure cooker with four cups of water and a teaspoon of salt. Cook for four to five minutes on full pressure and turn off the flame. Allow to cool. Open the cooker and keep the cooked beans ready to use in the stew.

In a large heavy-bottomed pot, heat the oil. Sauté bay leaves and garlic on a low flame for three to four minutes.

Add finely chopped onions and carrots. Sauté on a low flame for 10 minutes.

Chop the washed and cleaned green leafy vegetables. Add this to the pot and sauté on a high flame until the leaves wilt.

Mix in tomato puree, cumin, turmeric, red chilli powder and the remaining one teaspoon of salt.

Add the cooked beans with the liquid to the pot. Add two to three cups of boiling hot water to this mixture. Cover and cook for 15 minutes, allowing time for the beans to absorb all the flavours. Serve as is or with crusty bread or flatbreads.

Note: Seasonal vegetables like large cubes of sweet potato and pumpkin can also be added to the stew to make it even heartier.

*Buy the greens that are in season and available locally. Your local marketplace will have vendors that sell a variety of green leafy vegetables of which you can get a bunch each to use in this recipe.

MILLET SOYA BEAN KHICHDI

This is a powerhouse of a meal, super loaded with fibre and plant protein, and guaranteed to keep you full for many hours. I would recommend it for lunch or a heavy breakfast. Make sure the soya beans are pre-soaked for a minimum of eight hours so that they cook well.

Makes 3–4 servings

Ingredients

1 cup foxtail millet

⅓ - ½ cup soya beans, soaked overnight

1 ½ tsp salt

1 medium carrot

¼ cup green peas

½ cup chopped *methi* leaves (fenugreek leaves)

For the spice paste:
3 green chillies
5 cloves garlic
1–1½-inch piece of ginger
1 cup coriander leaves
3–4 tbsp grated fresh coconut

For the tempering:
1 tbsp ghee
1 tsp cumin seeds
1 pinch asafoetida

Method

Rinse and soak the millets in water for two to three hours.

Place the drained soya beans along with the drained millets in a pressure cooker. Add five cups of water. Pressure cook for 12 minutes (after full pressure, i.e., one whistle, keep the flame at a minimum for 12 minutes and then turn off). Once the pressure drops, open the cooker and season with salt along with ¼ cup hot water. Mix well.

Meanwhile, peel and dice the carrot. In a small pan, boil half a cup of water. Add diced carrot, green peas and *methi* leaves. Cover and simmer for six to seven minutes until the carrot is cooked.

Combine all the ingredients for the spice paste in a mixer jar and blend to a paste with two to three tablespoons of water.

Add the cooked vegetables and spice paste to the cooked millet-soya beans in the pressure cooker and bring the dish to a simmer.

Meanwhile, heat ghee in a small pan. Fry the cumin seeds. Once it splutters, stir in the asafoetida and remove from heat. Transfer the tempering over the *khichdi*. Serve hot with yoghurt and *amla* pickle.

Note: Use any other grains such as any variety of rice, amaranth or *bajra* instead of foxtail millet. Choose from a variety of beans such as black-eyed peas, green mung, moth beans, etc. Soaking time can be reduced to four hours for these beans. Use seasonal vegetables of your choice.

AMARANTH RISOTTO WITH ROASTED PUMPKIN

This Italian inspired dish is made using a local Indian grain. It makes for a fancy main course for dinner.

Makes 3–4 servings

Ingredients

For the amaranth:
1 cup amaranth seeds
1 tbsp butter
1 tbsp finely chopped garlic
½ cup finely chopped onion
2 ½ cups vegetable stock*

For the pumpkin:
1 tbsp olive oil
8–10 sage leaves or rosemary
1 tsp finely chopped garlic
2 cups diced pumpkin (~2 cm cubes)
Pinch of salt

Garnish:
2 tbsp butter
8–10 sage leaves

Method

Wash the amaranth seeds well and drain the water.

In a heavy-bottomed pan, heat butter and stir in the garlic and onion. Sauté on a low flame for eight minutes until the onion has softened. Add the drained amaranth seeds and sauté on a medium flame for two to three minutes.

Meanwhile, heat the stock in another pan and pour in hot vegetable stock, stirring constantly. Keep this on a low flame and stir intermittently until all the stock is absorbed and the amaranth grains are cooked. This should take around 20 minutes.

Additionally, prepare the pumpkin. In a pan, heat the olive oil. Fry the sage leaves for a few seconds. Add the chopped garlic and sauté on a low flame for 30 seconds. Add the pumpkin cubes and salt. Mix well and allow this to cook for 10–12 minutes until the pumpkin is tender and slightly golden brown around the edges.

For the garnish, heat the butter in a pan until it turns brown. Add in the sage leaves and turn off the flame.

To plate, serve two ladles of the risotto in a dish, making a small well in the centre. Serve two to three spoonfuls of the cooked pumpkin in the centre and top with half a tablespoon of the sage butter sauce. Serve this dish hot, as the amaranth will turn lumpy when cold.

*If there is a time constraint, dissolve two stock cubes in 2½ cups of boiling water. You can also use a mushroom stock instead of the vegetable stock. Mushrooms are a good alternative to the pumpkin as well. Choose the meaty milk mushrooms for this recipe.

MIXED DAL WITH MORINGA LEAVES

Dal is a staple in every Indian kitchen, be it to eat with roti or rice. In some form, it is prepared almost every day, making it a good vehicle to carry nutritious ingredients like DGLVs such as *moringa* leaves. By all means, try this recipe with one kind of dal, if it makes life easier. Adding a mix of dals is a good way to get different textures and a richer flavour in the dish.

Makes 6 servings

Ingredients

¼ cup *tur* dal
¼ cup chana dal
¼ cup *masoor* dal
¼ cup mung dal
2 cups *moringa* leaves
1 tsp turmeric powder

2 tbsp ghee
2 dried red chillies
1 pinch asafoetida
1 tsp cumin seeds
3 cloves
1 ½ tbsp ginger garlic paste
1 tsp red chilli powder
1 tsp garam masala powder

Garnish:
2–3 tbsp finely chopped coriander
Juice of a lime

Method

Wash the dals well and soak them in a bowl of water for 30 minutes. Drain and place in a pressure cooker with three cups of water along with *moringa* leaves and turmeric powder. Pressure cook for 10 minutes (after full pressure, i.e., one whistle, keep the flame at minimum for 10 minutes and turn off).

Meanwhile, prepare the tempering.

In a large pan, heat the ghee. Fry the red chillies. Stir in the asafoetida, cumin seeds and cloves. Once the seeds splutter and the cloves puff up, reduce the flame and fry the ginger garlic paste for a minute or so on a low flame until it no longer smells raw. Stir in the chilli powder along with a couple of tablespoons of water to prevent it from burning.

Mix the cooked dals into this. Stir to combine and finish by adding garam masala.

Remove the dish from the flame.

Garnish with coriander and lime juice just before serving with rice or rotis.

Note: This recipe can also be made using whole *urad* dal and *rajma* like a dal *makhani*. Sauté finely chopped onions and tomato puree along with the other ingredients (omit the cloves). Add cream towards the end.

SWEET POTATO AND BROWN RICE

This is starchy comfort food at its best. It also stays good in the refrigerator for two to three days and reheats well. Serve with a side of yoghurt or some sautéed paneer to give it the necessary protein boost.

Ingredients

2 medium sweet potatoes
1 tbsp coconut oil
1 tsp cumin seeds
1 tsp finely chopped green chillies
1 tsp finely chopped or grated ginger
1 cup finely chopped DGLVs
2 cups cooked brown rice (page 201)
½ tsp turmeric powder
½ tsp salt
¼ cup chopped coriander leaves
¼ cup roasted peanuts (unsalted)

Method

Scrub and wash the sweet potatoes well. Cut into centimetre-sized cubes.

Heat oil in a pan. Fry the cumin seeds until the seeds splutter. Reduce the flame and add the chillies and ginger. Sauté for a few seconds. Add the diced sweet potatoes and stir on a high flame for a minute or so until they are slightly golden on the outside. Reduce the flame and cook for five to six minutes until the sweet potato is cooked through. Mix in the chopped greens and sauté on high flame until the greens are wilted.

Stir in the cooked brown rice, turmeric and salt (if the rice is already salted while cooking, then reduce the salt used here).

Garnish with chopped coriander and crushed roasted peanuts just before serving.

CAULIFLOWER CABBAGE CARROT KOOTTU

This is a simple vegetable and lentil curry prepared in Tamil households on a regular basis using whichever vegetables are in season. Bottle gourd, peas, sweet potatoes and plantains are some of the many vegetables that can be used to prepare this *koottu*. When you have a little bit of every vegetable left over in the fridge, dice them all up and prepare a mixed vegetable *koottu* to clean out the fridge. The original recipe does not have sesame seeds, but it helps boost the nutrition profile of the recipe.

Makes 3–4 servings

Ingredients
2 medium carrots
5–6 broad beans
½ cup cauliflower florets (small)
¼ cup green peas
½ cup chopped cabbage
1 tsp salt
½ cup *tur* dal
¼ tsp turmeric

For the spice paste:
½ tsp oil
3 dried red chillies
1 tsp cumin seeds
1 tbsp sesame seeds
5 tbsp grated coconut (loosely packed)

For the tempering:
1 tbsp coconut oil
¼ tsp mustard seeds
1 sprig curry leaves
2 dried red chillies
½ tsp *urad* dal
Pinch of asafoetida

Method

Peel and dice the carrot into centimetre-sized cubes. De-string and chop the beans.

Soak the cauliflower florets in a bowl of salted water for 10 minutes. Remove the florets from the water, wash and drain well.

In a pan, heat one cup of water with a teaspoon of salt. Add the diced carrot. Cover and cook for five to seven minutes. To this, add the chopped cabbage, cauliflower florets, beans and peas and continue to simmer for six to seven minutes until all the vegetables are cooked, but retain their shape and texture.

While the vegetables are cooking, pressure cook the *tur* dal with one and a half cups of water and turmeric for 12-15 minutes on sim after the first whistle or full pressure. Once cooked, whisk it well. Mix the dal with the cooked vegetables in the pan.

To prepare the spice paste, heat half teaspoon of oil in a small pan. Fry the red chillies, cumin seeds and sesame seeds. Once the seeds splutter, turn off the flame. Transfer this to a mixer jar along with the grated coconut. Using ¼ cup water, grind this mix to a fine paste. Add the spice paste to the pan with the vegetables and dal. Bring the dish to a simmer, adjusting salt and water to get the consistency you like. Remove the *koottu* into a serving bowl.

Prepare the tempering by heating the oil in the same pan. Fry the mustard seeds, curry leaves, red chillies and *urad* dal. Once the dal turns golden brown, add the asafoetida and turn off the flame. Transfer the tempering over the *koottu* and keep covered until ready to serve.

SWEETS

AMARANTH FLOUR PINEAPPLE SHEERA

Sheera is usually made with whole wheat flour and served as a 'prasad' in some temples and for certain pujas. This version is made using amaranth flour and it uses the flavour and natural sweetness from ripe pineapples. You can also try it using ripe jackfruit or mangoes.

Makes 4–6 servings

Ingredients

2 tbsp ghee
1 cup amaranth flour
1 cup finely chopped pineapple
1 cup coarsely pureed pineapple
½ cup grated jaggery or raw cane sugar
2 cups water

To finish:
2 tbsp ghee
½ tsp ground green cardamom
Few saffron strands

Method

In a heavy-bottomed pan, heat ghee and roast the amaranth flour on low heat for around 10 minutes until you get a toasty aroma.

Meanwhile, in a saucepan, mix together chopped and pureéd pineapple, sugar and water. Bring to a simmer.

Once the flour is toasted, add the pineapple-sugar-water mixture to the flour, stirring constantly so that there are no lumps.

Cover and cook for six to eight minutes until all the water is absorbed and the flour is cooked.

Once the *sheera* is cooked, mix in the ghee and ground cardamom. Garnish with strands of saffron and serve hot.

SWEET POTATO HALWA

Naturally sweet and creamy mashed sweet potatoes make a perfect ingredient to make halwa. *Khoya* and besan give it the rich flavour that is a hallmark of many Indian sweets. This halwa is best made in winters when sweet potatoes are in season.
Makes 6 servings

Ingredients
3 tbsp ghee
1 cup mashed sweet potato
1 cup grated *khoya*
2 tbsp besan (roasted)
¾ cup raw cane sugar
¼ tsp green cardamom powder (seeds only)
3 tbsp finely chopped nuts (use a mix of almonds, pistas and cashews)
2 tbsp raisins

Method

Heat two tablespoons of ghee in a pan. Add the mashed sweet potato, *khoya*, besan and sugar. Mix well and keep stirring over a low flame for 10 minutes until it comes together and forms a ball. Sprinkle the green cardamom powder and stir well to combine. Remove to a bowl.

Separately, heat one tablespoon of ghee in the pan. Fry the chopped nuts and the raisins, until the raisins puff up and the nuts turn slightly golden brown. Transfer it on to the prepared halwa. Serve warm.

BUCKWHEAT DARK CHOCOLATE RAW BROWNIE BITES

These make for delicious sweet morsels to give your kids or work well as a post-dinner sweet bite for adults.

Makes 20 pieces

Ingredients
2 tbsp butter
½ cup buckwheat flour
½ cup chopped dark chocolate
½ cup almond flour
3–4 tbsp chopped almonds
½ cup raw cane sugar

1 tsp vanilla extract
2 tbsp cacao powder

Method

In a pan, heat the butter and add the buckwheat flour to the pan. Toast on a low flame until aromatic. This should take around 10 minutes.

In a dry microwave-safe bowl or a double boiler, melt the chocolate. In the microwave, this should take three to four bursts of 30 seconds each, stirring the chocolate in between.

To this, add the toasted buckwheat flour, almond flour, chopped nuts, sugar and vanilla and mix together. Cover with a cling film* and refrigerate for 30 minutes.

Spread out the mixture into a six-inch square pan lined with baking paper. Dust cacao powder over this using a sieve and refrigerate for one hour before cutting into small bite-sized squares.

Alternatively, use a tablespoon measuring spoon to scoop out the mixture and roll these into balls. Spread out cacao powder on a dish and roll each ball in the cacao powder.

Keep in the refrigerator in an airtight container.

Variation: Add a splash of flavourful liqueur like amaretto (almond) or Kahlua (coffee) to the mix before refrigerating.

*Try and use environmentally friendly and sustainable options like beeswax or silicone covers.

MILLET NUTMEG PAYASAM

Rice is traditionally used to make *kheer*. Varieties of millets such as foxtail millet, little millet and proso millet can be used to make *kheer* as they break down on slow cooking, giving thickness and creaminess to the *kheer*.

Makes 4 servings

Ingredients
⅓ cup little millet
1 litre whole milk
⅓ cup raw cane sugar
Nutmeg, for grating

Garnish:
1 tsp dried rose petals
2 tbsp chopped pistachios

Method

Wash and soak the millet in water for two hours.

Add milk to a heavy-bottomed pan. Bring to a boil and then simmer on a low flame for 20 minutes or so, stirring intermittently so it does not stick to the bottom of the pan. The milk should reduce by a third.

At this stage, add the sugar. Drain the soaked millets and add it to the milk.

Grate nutmeg to get two to three pinches worth and add it to the simmering milk.

Simmer for 20 to 25 minutes more until the millet is cooked and the *payasam* is thick.

Refrigerate for a few hours.

Serve chilled, garnished with rose petals and chopped pistachios.

The *payasam* can be prepared in an instant pot or slow cooker, by adding all the ingredients into the pot (except garnishes) and setting it to 'porridge' mode for 40 minutes. Chill the *payasam* and then garnish it.

DARK CHOCOLATE AVOCADO OLIVE OIL MOUSSE

Avocado is the best healthy ingredient to add to desserts. In one shot, this dessert gives the goodness of three nutrient and antioxidant-rich ingredients. It is rich in calories so enjoy it in smaller portions.

Makes 4 servings

Ingredients

½ cup chopped dark chocolate (70%)
1 ripe avocado
6 seedless dates*
2 tbsp maple syrup or honey
2 tbsp extra virgin olive oil
Pinch of coarse salt

*soak the dates in warm water for one hour if they are not the soft variety

Method

Melt the chocolate in a double boiler or a dry microwave-safe glass bowl. Run the microwave in 30 seconds bursts three times or so, stirring intermittently until the chocolate is melted.

Slice the avocado vertically around the stone. Twist the avocado to open and scoop out the stone with a spoon. Scoop out the flesh and place it in a mixer jar.

To this, add the dates, maple syrup and extra virgin olive oil. Blend to a smooth puree.

Scrape out this mixture with a silicone spatula into the melted chocolate. Fold together gently. Finish with a sprinkle of coarse salt.

Divide into four small glasses or serving bowls. Cover the bowls and refrigerate until set. You can also set the mousse in the mixing bowl itself. Sprinkle a few grains of coarse salt before serving.

CARROT SWEET POTATO CAKE

Another winter must-try is this hearty teacake stuffed with the goodness of vegetables like carrots and sweet potato. Mildly sweet, adequately spiced and richly flavoured with coconut oil, it makes a perfect accompaniment to your tea or coffee. You can also use this cake batter to make pancakes or waffles.

Makes 6–8 servings

Ingredients

½ cup whole wheat flour
½ cup amaranth flour
1 tsp baking powder
¼ tsp salt
¾ tsp ground cinnamon
½ tsp turmeric powder
1 egg*
½ cup raw cane sugar
4 tbsp coconut oil
2 tbsp desiccated coconut
½ cup packed finely grated carrot**
¼ cup mashed cooked sweet potato
3–4 tbsp milk

*As an alternative to egg, use a tablespoon of ground flaxseed in three tablespoons of boiling water. Whisk and keep in the fridge for 15 minutes before use.

**Use red carrots when in season as they are sweeter.

Method

Oil and prepare a six-inch round cake tin. Line with baking paper and keep aside.

Preheat oven at 180°C.

In a medium bowl, whisk the dry ingredients together until well combined.

In a large bowl, whisk together the egg, sugar and coconut oil, until well combined and frothy. To this, add the coconut, grated carrot and mashed sweet potato. Whisk to combine all these ingredients.

Add the dry ingredients to the combined wet ingredients and mix gently until no large lumps remain. Do not overmix the batter or the cake may turn out hard. If the batter seems too thick, add some or all of the milk to get a dropping consistency.

Scrape out the batter into the prepared pan and give it a tap on the counter. Keep the pan in the oven and bake for 35 minutes or so, until a skewer/tester comes out clean.

Remove and allow to cool in the pan for 10 minutes.

Run a knife around the circumference of the cake to loosen it from the sides of the pan. Turn over a wire rack and allow it to cool for another 30 minutes before slicing the cake.

Note: Grated apples or zucchinis can also be used instead of carrots. The moisture content of the vegetables used could vary, so adjust the batter consistency such that it is not too wet or dry.

RECIPE INDEX

Meal prep recipes

Beverages

3. Iced pineapple green tea (page 205)
4. Nutmeggy hot cocoa (page 205)
5. Wheatgrass black pepper honey shots (page 206)
6. Tamarind mint appetizer drink (page 206)
7. Turmeric ginger holy basil healing tea (page 207)
8. Boricha – Korean roasted barley tea (page 208)

Breakfast

1. Banana pineapple green tea smoothie (page 208)
2. Chocolate avocado cinnamon smoothie (page 209)
3. Popped amaranth chocolate granola (page 210)
4. Pineapple pomegranate yoghurt bowls (page 211)
5. Oats amla upma (page 211)
6. Buckwheat flour tomato dosas (page 212)
7. Millet surnoli (page 213)

Salads

1. Black-eyed peas, chargrilled corn and rocket salad (page 214)
2. Sweet potato chaat (page 216)
3. Amaranth salad (page 217)
4. Roasted pumpkin and massaged DGLV salad (page 218)
5. Red grapes and mung sprouts salad (page 220)
6. Broccoli, apple and walnut salad (page 221)
7. Avocado pomelo salad (page 222)
8. Roasted cauliflower with hung yoghurt dip (page 223)
9. Pomelo and betel leaf salad (page 224)

Mains

1. Black-eyed peas in ginger-garlic sauce (page 225)
2. Millets in tomato sauce parcels (page 227)
3. Sweet potato in tamarind sauce (Kuzhambu) (page 228)
4. Broccoli pakodis in kadhi (page 230)
5. Sprouted mung and pineapple curry (page 231)

6. Sweet potato buckwheat flatbread (page 232)
7. DGLV stew with black-eyed peas (page 234)
8. Millet soya bean khichdi (page 235)
9. Amaranth risotto with roasted pumpkin (page 237)
10. Mixed dal with moringa leaves (page 238)
11. Sweet potato and brown rice (page 240)
12. Cauliflower cabbage carrot kootttu (page 241)

Desserts

1. Amaranth flour pineapple sheera (page 242)
2. Sweet potato halwa (page 243)
3. Buckwheat dark chocolate raw brownie bites (page 244)
4. Millet nutmeg payasam (page 245)
5. Dark chocolate avocado olive oil mousse (page 246)
6. Carrot sweet potato cake (page 247)

Endnotes

Chapter 1

1. Maher L.A., Richter, T., Macdonald, D., D. Jones, M., Martin, L., Stock, J. 'Twenty Thousand-Year-Old Huts at a Hunter-Gatherer Settlement in Eastern Jordan'. PLOS ONE 7(2): e31447.
2. Koshy, J. *The Hindu.* 'Aliens in their own lands: when Chhattisgarh's tribals were turned into encroachers'. 6 April 2019.
3. Schaeffer, K. *Pew Research Center.* 'Among U.S. couples, women do more cooking and grocery shopping than men'. 2019.
4. Choudhari, P., & Desai, S. *Journal of Cleaner Production.* 'Gender inequalities and household fuel choice in India'. October 2019.
5. Warren, J.M., Smith, N., & Ashwell, M. *Nutrition Research Reviews.* 'A structured literature review on the role of mindfulness, mindful eating and intuitive eating in changing eating behaviours: effectiveness and associated potential mechanisms'. 30. 1-12. 18 July 2017.
6. Mishra, S. *Financial Express.* 'Coronavirus Impact: Demand for ready-to-eat foods gathers steam; sale increases by 20–30%'. 3 June 2020.

Chapter 2

1. *World Health Organization.* Mortality and global health estimates: Life expectancy and leading causes of death and disability. Available at: https://www.who.int/gho/

mortality_burden_disease/life_tables/situation_trends_text/en/
2. *World Health Organization.* The impact of chronic disease in India. Available at: https://www.who.int/chp/chronic_disease_report/media/india.pdf?ua=1
3. Harvard Health Publishing. *Harvard Men's Health Watch.* 'Understanding acute and chronic inflammation'. Available at: https://www.health.harvard.edu/staying-healthy/understanding-acute-and-chronic-inflammation

Chapter 3

1. Fitzgerald, M. 'It's a Bird! It's a Plane! It's Superfood!'. *Diet Cults: The Surprising Fallacy at the Core of Nutrition Fads and a Guide to Healthy Eating for the Rest of Us.* Pegasus Books. 2014.

Chapter 4

1. Elbein, S. *Texas Observer.* 'The Seeds That Time Forgot'. 17 April 2013.
2. Gusain, R. *Daily Mail Online India.* 'Uttarakhand farmers turn to Amaranth crop as flour makes a comeback'. 1 December 2014.
3. D'souza, J. J., D'souza, P. P., Fazal, F., Kumar, A., Bhat, H. P., & Baliga, M. S. 'Anti-diabetic effects of the Indian indigenous fruit Emblica officinalis Gaertn: active constituents and modes of action'. *Food & function*, *5*(4), 635–644. 2014.
4. Zhao, T., Sun, Q., Marques, M., & Witcher, M. Anticancer Properties of Phyllanthus emblica (Indian Gooseberry). *Oxidative medicine and cellular longevity.* 2015.
5. Uchiyama, T., Tsunenaga, M., Miyanaga, M., Ueda, O., & Ogo, M. Oral intake of lingonberry and amla fruit extract improves skin conditions in healthy female subjects: A randomized, double-blind, placebo-controlled clinical trial. *Biotechnology and applied biochemistry*, *66*(5), 870–879. 2019.
6. Ahmed, N., Tcheng, M., Roma, A., Buraczynski, M., Jayanth, P., Rea, K., Akhtar, T. A., & Spagnuolo, P. A. Avocatin B

Protects Against Lipotoxicity and Improves Insulin Sensitivity in Diet-Induced Obesity. *Molecular nutrition & food research, 63*(24), e1900688. 2019.

7. Fulgoni, V. L., 3rd, Dreher, M., & Davenport, A. J. Avocado consumption is associated with better diet quality and nutrient intake, and lower metabolic syndrome risk in US adults: results from the National Health and Nutrition Examination Survey (NHANES) 2001-2008. *Nutrition journal, 12*, 1. 2013.
8. Sen, S., Dayanandan, S., Davis, T., Ganesan, R., Jagadish, M.R., Mathew, P.J., Ravikanth, G. Origin and evolution of the genus *Piper* in Peninsular India. *Molecular Phylogenetics and Evolution*. Vol. 138. 2 November 2018.
9. Kharbanda, C., Alam, M. S., Hamid, H., Javed, K., Bano, S., Ali, Y., Dhulap, A., Alam, P., & Pasha, M. A. Novel Piperine Derivatives with Antidiabetic Effect as PPAR-γ Agonists. *Chemical biology & drug design, 88*(3), 354–362. 2016.
10. Li, Y., Zhang, T., Korkaya, H., Liu, S., Lee, H. F., Newman, B., Yu, Y., Clouthier, S. G., Schwartz, S. J., Wicha, M. S., & Sun, D. Sulforaphane, a dietary component of broccoli/broccoli sprouts, inhibits breast cancer stem cells. *Clinical cancer research: an official journal of the American Association for Cancer Research, 16*(9), 2580–2590. 2010.
11. Anand David, A. V., Arulmoli, R., & Parasuraman, S. Overviews of Biological Importance of Quercetin: A Bioactive Flavonoid. *Pharmacognosy reviews, 10*(20), 84–89. 2016.
12. Soundararajan, P., & Kim, J. S. Anti-Carcinogenic Glucosinolates in Cruciferous Vegetables and Their Antagonistic Effects on Prevention of Cancers. *Molecules (Basel, Switzerland), 23*(11), 2983. 2018.
13. Zaini, R., Clench, M. R., & Le Maitre, C. L. Bioactive chemicals from carrot (Daucus carota) juice extracts for the treatment of leukemia. *Journal of medicinal food, 14*(11), 1303–1312. 2011.
14. Oude Griep, L., Monique Verschuren, W., Kromhout, D., Ocké, M., & Geleijnse, J. Colours of fruit and

vegetables and 10-year incidence of CHD. *British Journal of Nutrition, 106*(10), 1562-1569. 2011.

15. Kapusta-Duch, Joanna & Kopeć, Aneta & Piątkowska, Ewa & Borczak, Barbara & Leszczyńska, Teresa. The beneficial effects of Brassica vegetables on human health. *Roczniki Państwowego Zakładu Higieny.* 63. 389-95. 2012.
16. Ludovici, V., Barthelmes, J., Nägele, M. P., et al. Cocoa, Blood Pressure, and Vascular Function. *Frontiers in Nutrition.* 2 August 2017.
17. Ramos, S., Martin, M.A., & Goya, L. Effects of Cocoa Antioxidants in Type 2 Diabetes Mellitus. *Antioxidants (Basel, Switzerland), 6*(4), 84. 31 October 2017.
18. Nehlig A. The neuroprotective effects of cocoa flavanol and its influence on cognitive performance. *British journal of clinical pharmacology, 75*(3), 716–727. 2013.
19. Lin, H. L., An, Q. Z., Wang, Q. Z., & Liu, C. X. Folate intake and pancreatic cancer risk: an overall and dose-response meta-analysis. *Public Health.* 2013.

20. Cordero-Herrera, I., Kozyra, M., Zhuge, Z., Haworth, S.M., Moretti, C., et al. AMP-activated protein kinase activation and NADPH oxidase inhibition by inorganic nitrate and nitrite prevent liver steatosis. *Proceedings of the National Academy of Sciences.* 2 January 2019.
21. Al-Shwyeh H. A. Date Palm (*Phoenix dactylifera* L.) Fruit as Potential Antioxidant and Antimicrobial Agents. *Journal of pharmacy & bioallied sciences, 11*(1), 1–11. 2019.
22. Al-Shwyeh H. A. Date Palm (*Phoenix dactylifera* L.) Fruit as Potential Antioxidant and Antimicrobial Agents. U.S. *National Library of Medicine. 2019.*
23. Touillaud, M. S., Thiébaut, A. C., Fournier, A., Niravong, M., Boutron-Ruault, M. C., & Clavel-Chapelon, F. Dietary lignan intake and postmenopausal breast cancer risk by estrogen and progesterone receptor status. *Journal of the National Cancer Institute, 99*(6), 475–486. 2007.
24. Omar, S. H., & Al-Wabel, N. A. Organosulfur compounds and possible mechanism of garlic in cancer. *Saudi pharmaceutical*

journal: SPJ: the official publication of the Saudi Pharmaceutical Society, 18(1), 51–58. 2010.

25. Hoseinzadeh, K., Daryanoosh, F., Baghdasar, P. J., & Alizadeh, H. Acute effects of ginger extract on biochemical and functional symptoms of delayed onset muscle soreness. *Medical journal of the Islamic Republic of Iran, 29*, 261. 2015.
26. Rahnama, P., Montazeri, A., Huseini, H. F., Kianbakht, S., & Naseri, M. Effect of Zingiber officinale R. rhizomes (ginger) on pain relief in primary dysmenorrhea: a placebo randomized trial. *BMC complementary and alternative medicine, 12*, 92. 2012.
27. Tang, D., Dong, Y., Ren, H., Li, L., & He, C. A review of phytochemistry, metabolite changes, and medicinal uses of the common food mung bean and its sprouts (Vigna radiata). *Chemistry Central journal, 8*(1), 4. 2014.
28. Li, W., 2014. *Can We Starve Cancer?*. [Youtube]. Available at: https://www.youtube.com/watch?v=OjkzfeJz66o
29. Kuriyama, S., Shimazu, T., Ohmori, K., Kikuchi, N., Nakaya, N., Nishino, Y., Tsubono, Y., & Tsuji, I. Green tea consumption and mortality due to cardiovascular disease, cancer, and all causes in Japan: the Ohsaki study. *JAMA, 296*(10), 1255–1265. 2006.
30. Napoli, C., & Ignarro, L. J. Nitric oxide and pathogenic mechanisms involved in the development of vascular diseases. *Archives of pharmacal research, 32*(8), 1103–1108. 2009.
31. Chang, C. S., Sun, H. L., Lii, C. K., Chen, H. W., Chen, P. Y., & Liu, K. L. Gamma-linolenic acid inhibits inflammatory responses by regulating NF-kappaB and AP-1 activation in lipopolysaccharide-induced RAW 264.7 macrophages. *Inflammation, 33*(1), 46–57. 2010.
32. Touillaud, M. S., Thiébaut, A. C., Fournier, A., Niravong, M., Boutron-Ruault, M. C., & Clavel-Chapelon, F. Dietary lignan intake and postmenopausal breast cancer risk by estrogen and progesterone receptor status. *Journal of the National Cancer Institute, 99*(6), 475–486. 2007.

33. Gopalakrishnan, L., Doriya, K., Santhosh Kumar, D. Moringa oleifera: A review on nutritive importance and its medicinal application. *Food Science and Human Wellness.* June 2016.
34. Subbiah, K. A., & Balan, V. A Comprehensive Review of Tropical Milky White Mushroom (Calocybe indica P&C). *Mycobiology*, *43*(3), 184–194. 2015.
35. Roupas, P., Keogh, J., Noakes, M., Margetts, C., Taylor, P. Mushrooms and agaritine: A mini-review. Journal of Functional Foods. April 2010.
36. Boots, A. W., Haenen, G. R., & Bast, A. Health effects of quercetin: from antioxidant to nutraceutical. *European journal of pharmacology*, *585*(2-3), 325–337. 2008.
37. Asgary, S., Keshvari, M., Sahebkar, A., & Sarrafzadegan, N. Pomegranate Consumption and Blood Pressure: A Review. *Current pharmaceutical design*, *23*(7), 1042–1050. 2017.
38. Paller, C. J., Pantuck, A., & Carducci, M. A. A review of pomegranate in prostate cancer. *Prostate cancer and prostatic diseases*, *20*(3), 265–270. 2017.

39. Zhou, Y., Wang, T., Meng, Q., & Zhai, S. Association of carotenoids with risk of gastric cancer: A meta-analysis. *Clinical nutrition (Edinburgh, Scotland)*, *35*(1), 109–116. 2016.
40. J. Zunino, S. Type 2 Diabetes and Glycemic Response to Grapes or Grape Products. *The Journal of Nutrition.* Vol. 139, Issue 9. September 2009.
41. Federation of Indian Chambers of Commerce & Industry (FICCI). 2015. *Evaluation of the PPIAD Project on Soybean.* Retrieved from SOYBEAN Report: http://ficci.in/spdocument/20539/SOYBEAN-Report.pdf
42. Chen, M. N., Lin, C. C., & Liu, C. F. Efficacy of phytoestrogens for menopausal symptoms: a meta-analysis and systematic review. *Climacteric: the journal of the International Menopause Society*, *18*(2), 260–269. 2015.
43. Lila, M.A. Anthocyanins and Human Health: An In Vitro Investigative Approach. *Journal of Biomedical Biotechnology.* 306-313. 1 Dec 2004.

44. Guo, S., Ge, Y., & Na Jom, K. A review of phytochemistry, metabolite changes, and medicinal uses of the common sunflower seed and sprouts (Helianthus annuus L.). *Chemistry Central journal, 11*(1), 95. 2017.
45. Komakech, R., Kim, Y.G., Matsabisa, G.M., Kang, Y. Anti-inflammatory and analgesic potential of *Tamarindus indica* Linn. (Fabaceae): a narrative review. *Integrative Medicine Research Journal.* 181-186. Sep 2019.
46. Sundaram, M. S., Hemshekhar, M., Santhosh, M. S., Paul, M., Sunitha, K., Thushara, R. M., NaveenKumar, S. K., Naveen, S., Devaraja, S., Rangappa, K. S., Kemparaju, K., & Girish, K. S. Tamarind Seed (Tamarindus indica) Extract Ameliorates Adjuvant-Induced Arthritis via Regulating the Mediators of Cartilage/Bone Degeneration, Inflammation and Oxidative Stress. *Scientific reports, 5,* 11117. 2015.
47. Cornell University. (2002, April 23). Cooking Tomatoes Boosts Disease-Fighting Power. *ScienceDaily.* Retrieved November 21, 2020 from www.sciencedaily.com/releases/2002/04/020422073341.htm
48. Funk, J. L., Oyarzo, J. N., Frye, J. B., Chen, G., Lantz, R. C., Jolad, S. D., Sólyom, A. M., & Timmermann, B. N. Turmeric extracts containing curcuminoids prevent experimental rheumatoid arthritis. *Journal of natural products, 69*(3), 351–355. 2006.
49. Nakagawa, Y., Mukai, S., Yamada, S., Matsuoka, M., Tarumi, E., Hashimoto, T., Tamura, C., Imaizumi, A., Nishihira, J., & Nakamura, T. Short-term effects of highly-bioavailable curcumin for treating knee osteoarthritis: a randomized, double-blind, placebo-controlled prospective study. *Journal of orthopaedic science: official journal of the Japanese Orthopaedic Association, 19*(6), 933–939. 2014.
50. Fu, Z., Chen, X., Guan, S., Yan, Y., Lin, H., & Hua, Z. C. Curcumin inhibits angiogenesis and improves defective hematopoiesis induced by tumor-derived VEGF in tumor model through modulating VEGF-VEGFR2 signaling pathway. *Oncotarget, 6*(23), 19469–19482. 2015.

51. Mishra, S., Palanivelu, K. The effect of curcumin (turmeric) on Alzheimer's disease: An overview. Annals of Indian Academy of Neurology. 13-19. 2008.
52. D Allerton, T., N. Proctor, D., M. Stephens, J., R. Dugas, T., Spielmann, G., A. Irving, B. l-Citrulline Supplementation: Impact on Cardiometabolic Health. *Nutrients*. 2018 Jul 19.
53. Gore, R. D., Palaskar, S. J., & Bartake, A. R. Wheatgrass: Green Blood can Help to Fight Cancer. *Journal of clinical and diagnostic research: JCDR, 11*(6), ZC40–ZC42. 2017.
54. Bar-Sela, G., Cohen, M., Ben-Arye, E., Epelbaum, R. The Medical Use of Wheatgrass: Review of the Gap Between Basic and Clinical Applications. *Mini-Reviews in Medicinal Chemistry*. 2015.

Chapter 5

1. Nugent, A.P. Health properties of resistant starch. *Nutrition Bulletin*. 30: 27-54. Mar 2005.
2. Azab, M. Gut Bacteria Can Influence Your Mood, Thoughts, and Brain. 2019 Aug 7. Retrieved from Psychology Today: https://www.psychologytoday.com/us/blog/neuroscience-in-everyday-life/201908/gut-bacteria-can-influence-your-mood-thoughts-and-brain
3. Stonehouse, W. Does Consumption of LC Omega-3 PUFA Enhance Cognitive Performance in Healthy School-Aged Children and throughout Adulthood? Evidence from Clinical Trials. *Nutrients*. 2730-2758. 2014 Jul 22.
4. Montgomery, P., Burton, J.R., Sewell, R.P., Spreckelsen, T.F., & Richardson, A.J. Fatty acids and sleep in UK children: subjective and pilot objective sleep results from the DOLAB study – a randomized controlled trial. *Journal of Sleep Research*. 364-388. 2014 Aug.

Chapter 6

1. Diego Quintaes, K., Haj-Isa, N.M., Trezza Netto, J., & Amaya-Farfan, J., Soapstone utensils may improve iron status in adult women. A preliminary study. *Archivos latinoamericanos de nutricion*. 429-432. 2011 Dec.

Chapter 7

1. Moynihan, Q. *Business Insider*. 'How veganism may one day become unsustainable'. 2018.
2. Food and Agriculture Organization of the United Nations. *Sustainable diets and Biodiversity - Directions and solutions for policy, research and action.* 2012. Retrieved from Food and Agriculture Organization: http://www.fao.org/3/i3004e/i3004e00.htm
3. Naylor, T. *The Guardian*. Ditch the almond milk: why everything you know about sustainable eating is probably wrong'. 2018.
4. Yu, L. *Global Food, Health, And Society*. 'Superfoods' Dark Side: Increasing Vulnerability of Quinoa Farmers in Bolivia'. 22 January 2019.
5. Chainey, R. 2015 August 13. *Which countries waste the most food?* Retrieved from World Economic Forum: https://www.weforum.org/agenda/2015/08/which-countries-waste-the-most-food/
6. Leavens, M. 2017 March 7. *Do food miles really matter?* Retrieved from Harvard University | Sustainability: https://green.harvard.edu/news/do-food-miles-really-matter
7. Singh, Ram. *Facebook*. Available here: https://www.facebook.com/photo?fbid=10218372001068113&set=a.2218206731423

Bibliography

1. Pastor, K., Acanski, M. The chemistry behind amaranth grains. Journal of Nutritional Health & Food Engineering. 8(5):358-360. 2018 Oct 12.
2. National Research Council. 2006. *Lost Crops of Africa: Volume II: Vegetables.* Washington, DC: The National Academies Press.
3. Kuru, P. Tamarindus indica and its health related effects. *Asian Pacific Journal of Tropical Biomedicine.* Vol. 4, Issue 9. 676-681. Sept 2014.
4. Arshad, M.S., Imran, M., Ahmed, A., et al. Tamarind: A diet-based strategy against lifestyle maladies. *Food Science Nutrition.* 7: 3378– 3390. 27 Sept 2019.
5. Bar-Sela, G., Cohen, M., Ben-Arye, E., & Epelbaum, R. The Medical Use of Wheatgrass: Review of the Gap Between Basic and Clinical Applications. *Mini reviews in medicinal chemistry, 15*(12), 1002–1010. 2015.
6 Ramos, S. C., Fonseca, F. A., Kasmas, S. H., Moreira, F. T., Helfenstein, T., Borges, N. C., Moreno, R. A., Rezende, V. M., Silva, F. C., & Izar, M. C. The role of soluble fiber intake in patients under highly effective lipid-lowering therapy. *Nutrition journal, 10*, 80. 2011.
7. Salas-Salvadó, J., Farrés, X., Luque, X., Narejos, S., Borrell, M., Basora, J., Anguera, A., Torres, F., Bulló, M., Balanza, R., & Fiber in Obesity-Study Group Effect of two doses of a mixture of soluble fibres on body weight and metabolic variables in overweight or obese patients: a randomised trial. *The British journal of nutrition, 99*(6), 1380–1387. 2008.

8. Lyte, M. Microbial Endocrinology in the Microbiome-Gut-Brain Axis: How Bacterial Production and Utilization of Neurochemicals Influence Behavior. *PLos Pathogens*. 9(11). 2015.
9. Zhang, Y. J., Li, S., Gan, R. Y., Zhou, T., Xu, D. P., & Li, H. B. Impacts of gut bacteria on human health and diseases. *International journal of molecular sciences, 16*(4), 7493–7519. 2015.
10. FRLHT's ENVIS Resource Partner on Medicinal Plants. (n.d.). Retrieved from ENVIS Centre on Medicinal Plants: https://envis.frlht.org/
11. Füleky, G. *Cultivated Plants, Primarily as Food Sources*. EOLSS Publishers.
12. Mason, P. *Royal Society of Arts*. 'What is a Sustainable Diet and Why Do We Need It?' 20 May 2018.
13. Peters, C.J., Picardy, J., Darrouzet-Nardi, A.F., Wilkins, J.L., Griffin, T.S., & Fick, G.W. Carrying capacity of U.S. agricultural land: Ten diet scenarios. *Elementa: Science of the Anthropocene*. 2016.
14. Ackers, K. *Eco&Beyond*. 'What Does Food Sustainability Really Mean?' (n.d.).

Acknowledgments

I'll start by thanking my husband, Sumanth, who has always pushed me to follow my dreams and continuously inspires me with his discipline and dedication towards his work and ultrarunning. Working from home for most of 2020, he took on a lot of my responsibilities, allowing me to focus fully on this book.

My son Atri, who is my no.1 food taster and provider of nuanced feedback on the dishes (only when asked). He was very understanding this past year, letting me write and edit undisturbed even though he was bored out of his wits being home all the time during this pandemic, while also making me cups of the best ginger tea to keep me going.

My mother and my maternal aunts, whose blessings and encouragement mean everything to me.

My food content creator friends on social media, who wow me with their creativity every single day.

My zen-like editor Prerna, who found me to be cool enough to work with me a second time.

Lastly – and very importantly – the new pup in my life, Ida, who, despite stealing all the carrots in the house, gives me many playful moments in which I feel like a child again.

About the Author

Nandita Iyer is a medical doctor who specializes in nutrition, and is a seasoned columnist. She has written on nutrition, health and food for over 15 years. She is the author of the popular blog Saffron Trail and the bestselling book *The Everyday Healthy Vegetarian*. She has been featured in and has written for BBC *Good Food, Vogue, Femina* and *India Today*, among other publications.

When not experimenting in the kitchen or writing, she loves pottering in her kitchen garden and singing Hindustani classical music.

Nandita lives in Bengaluru with her husband and son. You can follow her on Twitter and Instagram at @saffrontrail.